COMPILE YOUR DREAMS

Every Dream Deserves To Run Without Errors

MASTERING EMBEDDED SYSTEMS DEVELOPMENT

A STORY-DRIVEN GUIDE FOR ENGINEERS, STUDENTS & MAKERS

SATEESH BAGANAL

Clever Fox® PUBLISHING

Chennai • Bangalore

CLEVER FOX PUBLISHING
Chennai, India

Published by CLEVER FOX PUBLISHING 2025

ISBN: 978-93-6707-514-2

Dedication

To **Amma and Appa—**

Your quiet sacrifices empower every page of this book.

To **my brother —**

For always being the silent supporter, the first believer, and the one who reminded me without words that family is the backbone of every ambition.

To **my wife –**

For being my quiet strength, my calm in the chaos, and the one who stood beside me through every late night, every setback, and every small step forward. Your unwavering belief gave me the courage to keep going.

To my first **team—**

Thank you for placing your faith in a lead who was still finding his footing. Together, we turned long nights and failed attempts into lessons, and lessons into triumphs.

To the **mentors** *who nurtured my curiosity before I even understood the craft.*

And to every **aspiring engineer** *holding this book—*

May these stories illuminate your path, just as your silent determination has always inspired mine.

Dedication

CONTENTS

WHY THIS BOOK IS DIFFERENT?

Most embedded systems books teach you the "what" and "how" in isolation. They give you a set of commands, code snippets, and diagrams. But they rarely show you the life behind the code, the struggles behind the solutions, or the human journey that shapes a real engineer.

This book stands apart from all others.

Technical concepts are not simply dropped on you by it. You are taken inside the story of building a real embedded project, progressing from blinking an LED to deploying a fully functional system. You are reading about more than just I2C, RTOS, or kernel debugging. Living through them is what you are doing. A team that laughs, argues, burns boards, and celebrates breakthroughs together.

Here is what you will learn:

- **The complete embedded development lifecycle** — requirement gathering, design, drivers, debugging, optimisation, testing, deployment, and maintenance.
- **How theory meets reality** — when things go wrong, deadlines slip. You must be ready to respond to the unexpected.
- **The mindset shift** from being just a coder to becoming an embedded systems engineer who understands the system.

This is the first embedded systems book that blends technical mastery with real-world storytelling, so you remember concepts not as dry definitions, but as a lived experience.

By the end, you will not only know how embedded systems work, but you will have the mindset, confidence, and resilience to build systems that matter. Face challenges without fear and grow into the engineer you always wanted to be.

This is not simply a book.

It is a new way of learning, one that can transform your skills, your career, and the way you see engineering.

"More than reading, you should engage with this book."

ABOUT THE AUTHOR

– Sateesh Baganal

With a foundation built on real-world challenges, **Sateesh Baganal** brings practical insight to embedded systems beyond textbook theory. He learned about embedded systems extensively, immersing himself in the subject.

With hands-on experience in microcontrollers, Linux systems, kernel internals, RTOS, and real-world product development, Sateesh has worked across various domains, including healthcare, aviation, defence, and IoT. What sets him apart is his ability to translate complex engineering principles into relatable experiences and to turn every setback into a stepping stone.

Beyond the labs and terminals, he is a mentor, educator, and motivator who believes in the power of **self-study**, **team spirit**, and **curiosity-driven learning**. His passion for teaching, paired with his technical expertise, led him to create this book not just to share knowledge but to light the path for others.

Through ***Compile Your Dreams***, Sateesh hopes to inspire students, engineers, educators, and dreamers to look beyond tutorials and tools and instead embrace the real stories behind learning, failure, growth, and success.

AUTHOR'S NOTE

In a world that is rushing toward automation. I have learned that machines cannot replicate persistent curiosity. AI can guide you, even amaze you. But when the tools go silent, it is your insight that shows the way.

AI is your accelerator, not your engine. Your real engine is self-study.

"AI suggests. You decide. Use it like a smart junior, not a magical fix. The creativity, context, and quality still come from us."

So, do not just use tools, build your own mind. That is the only tool that never goes obsolete.

Self-Study Builds What AI Can't:

- **Confidence** to stand without a crutch.
- **Creativity** to explore beyond given solutions.
- **Clarity** that survives any exam, interview, or production bug.
- **Character** that turns failures into fuel.

"Tools can speed up learning, but only effort turns it into understanding."

FOREWORD

In the world of engineering, we often celebrate the finished project, passing tests, and production deployments. But do we discuss the chaos behind the scenes, the uncertainty, the late nights, the broken boards, the self-doubt?

That is where this book begins, not with perfection, but with **possibility**.

Sateesh's journey is about more than building embedded systems—it is about building belief.

Through this personal and rich narrative, he walks us through the beautiful process of learning and taking ownership.

What makes this book so special is that it never loses sight of **the human behind the hardware**. Each chapter does more than teach; It connects. It reminds us that engineering is more than code and datasheets. That concerns personal and group development.

Whether you are a student, a curious beginner, or a professional seeking direction, this book will meet you where you are and take you somewhere better. You will find yourself nodding, smiling, sometimes even tearing up as you recognise pieces of your own journey reflected in these pages.

By the end, your learning will extend beyond C programming, protocols, and Linux internals. You will learn **resilience, teamwork, and how to lead even when you are unsure**.

PREFACE

When I began this journey, I did not imagine it would one day become a story worth telling—one with long commutes, sleepless nights, burnt boards, and quiet victories. I was not born an expert. I wondered with an insatiable curiosity about the inner workings of machines, moving data, and the potential of even the smallest component.

Today, we have AI tools at our fingertips intelligent, fast, and helpful. And yes, I use them too. But through all this, one truth has stayed with me:

AI can assist. But self-study transforms.

Experience alone teaches some lessons. You learn some lessons from only failure; books do not contain all lessons. One kernel panic had me unravel every line of the DTS until I understood the hardware's language. Debugging taught me patience. Falling in front of my team taught me resilience. And every setback became a stepping stone toward mastery.

Curiosity kept me going. No shortcuts. No quick fix.

To all readers, whether students, professionals, or beginners, the message is clear: Use this book as a roadmap but let your passion lead the way. Use tools wisely, but build the core within you through deliberate learning and a relentless desire to understand.

Because one day, someone will look at you, not the code and say, "**You're the one who made this work.**" And then, you will understand why it was all worthwhile.

EDITION NOTE

This is the initial release of a book with a purpose beyond a typical book.

It started as scattered notes, debug logs, team chats, and the quiet reflections of a junior engineer learning the hard way. What you hold in your hands today is the refined outcome of those raw experiences. Organised not only to teach you concepts but to help you feel the journey of embedded development.

As this edition comes to life, I have done my best to ensure that each chapter balances technical depth with real-world context. Still, engineering grows, and so will this book. Future editions will grow with new insights, updated tools, real deployment stories, and contributions from readers and engineers like you.

If you find areas for improvement, or if this book helped you in any way, I invite you to connect with me. Your feedback will guide the next release and help shape a resource that grows with its community.

Thank you for being part of **this first step**.

HOW TO GET THE MOST OUT OF THIS BOOK

Each chapter introduces critical embedded concepts like:

- C programming and microcontroller architecture.
- Linux internals and boot process.
- RTOS and communication protocols.
- IPC, debugging, build systems, testing, profiling, and more.

To really gain from it, do not only read it. Live it.

Here is how:

1. **Follow the Story, Absorb the Lessons**
   Every chapter begins with a real-world scenario, a story that mirrors the challenges engineers face. Let the story draw you in, then connect the dots with the technical insights that follow.
2. **Do not Skip the Technical Notes**
   Stories inspire, but notes empower. After each major section, you will find **simplified explanations, diagrams, and code references**. These are your quick guides for practice and review.
3. **Learn by Doing**
   Whenever you see code, replicate it. Break it. Fix it. Modify it. The fastest way to learn embedded systems is by getting your hands dirty.

4. **Build Alongside the Book**
   Set up a small lab, a microcontroller board, and a Linux machine. The magic happens when theory meets hardware in your hands.
5. **Pause and Reflect**
   Some chapters end with questions or challenges. Do not rush through them; these reflections strengthen problem-solving skills.
6. **Revisit Chapters During Projects**
   Treat this book as a mentor in print. When you are stuck during real work, come back to the relevant chapter for guidance.
7. **Keep a Learning Journal**
   Note down the errors you faced, the fixes you found, and the concepts that clicked. Your personal notes will become your strongest resource.
8. **Stay Curious, Always**
   This is not just about embedded systems. It is about building the mindset of an engineer. Every "why" you ask will make you better than yesterday.

Let us get started.

The first bug is waiting to be discovered, and so is your potential.

So, keep turning the page. **Your journey might just begin here.**

HOW DREAMS SHAPE THE LIFE WE LIVE

The Spark That Started It All

Well before I typed my first line of code or felt the weight of a multimeter. I was just a curious kid, staring wide-eyed at machines that blinked, buzzed, and moved with purpose. My earliest memory? Watching the old washing machine at home. Its noise did not fascinate me, but it is the timing of stopping. How the timer operated, how water flowed at the right moment.

I began asking questions that no one nearby could answer.

"Who tells the fan to turn off when the room is cool?"

"How does the TV remote work without wires?"

"How does a microwave determine a food's completion?

Back then, I was unfamiliar with the term "embedded systems." But I understood these were not ordinary machines; they had something inside that made them smart. That "something" became my obsession.

In school, I would take apart broken toys, old radios, and remote-control cars not to fix them, but to understand them. I would sit for hours, looking at the tiny chips and wires, trying to guess what each part did. Many times, I failed to put them back together, but I always walked away with one new clue.

Curiosity Comes with a Cost

I remember one afternoon. A neighbour's kid had just shown off a brand-new remote-control car. Sleek, fast, shiny red. Everyone wanted a turn racing it across the dusty front yard. But while others raced it, I watched the wheels, the antenna, the little switch on the underside.

A few hours later, when no one was looking, I asked, "Can I see it?"

The boy nodded.

Ten minutes later, I had the whole thing opened, wires spread out like spaghetti, screws rolling under the table, circuit board flipped in my lap.

I wondered. **What made it turn ON? How did the antenna talk to the wheels?** But before I could figure it out… I heard it.

"SATEESH!"

It was Amma. And she was not alone—Appa was right behind her.

The scolding came fast and loud.

"Why would you open someone else's toy? Do you think money grows on trees?"

"Every week you break something—the TV remote last time, now this!"

My heart pounded as I stood frozen, hands still holding the toy's shell. I had no intention of destroying anything. Driven by curiosity, I needed to understand its mechanics.

Their anger was a palpable thing that day. So, but later, Amma sat beside me and said something I never forgot:

"If you're going to open things, Sateesh, you'd better grow up and learn how to put them back."

And I did. I started learning the names of components, how circuits flowed, and how not to rip off connectors. I still made mistakes, but I also fixed things. Remote. Doorbell. FM radio. I even helped my teacher fix a lab instrument in high school.

I had broken things out of curiosity, but it was those same broken things that shaped my purpose.

The Spark of Motivation: Becoming an Embedded Engineer

From the very beginning, I was fascinated by how small devices could do big things. As a child, I would break apart toys not to destroy them, but to see what made them *alive*. My parents scolded me often for leaving behind broken plastic and wires, but inside me, curiosity was stronger than fear. I wanted to know *why* and *how*.

That curiosity only grew during my university days. I still remember the lecture when a professor explained that microcontrollers were not just chips. They were at the heart of devices that saved lives. Pacemakers, infusion pumps, ventilators — all powered by embedded systems. For the first time, I realised that code and circuits were not just technical puzzles. They were lifelines.

Then came aviation. Reading how autopilots, navigation systems, and sensors worked seamlessly at 35,000 feet lit another fire in me. The idea that one embedded failure could risk hundreds of lives, but one flawless design could save them, was both terrifying and deeply motivating.

Defence added another layer. Embedded systems in radar, secure communication, and guidance systems made me think: *What if I could use my skills to contribute to my country's safety?*

Even in daily life — cars, phones, home automation- I saw proof that embedded systems were everywhere. And I knew I wanted to be part of that invisible army of engineers shaping the world from behind the scenes.

But my journey was not easy. There were rejections, self-doubts, nights spent debugging boards, long commutes, and even moments when quitting seemed tempting. Yet, every failure became a lesson. Every burnt board, every kernel panic, every scolding from a manager became fuel. Slowly, I realised that embedded systems were not just my career; they were my calling.

Today, when I look back, I see how every challenge shaped me. Embedded systems taught me persistence, curiosity, and resilience. And that is why I chose this path: not just to code, but to create systems that matter.

This book is not only my story; it is an invitation. To every aspiring engineer reading this: may you discover your spark, may you endure your challenges, and may you find joy in the unseen victories of an embedded engineer's life.

A Vision for the Future

I see how each of these domains' healthcare, aviation, defence, and real-time products shaped my vision of what I wanted to achieve as an embedded engineer. I desired to be more than a coder.

The difficulties were significant; however, the opportunities matched that magnitude. Within the gap between hardship and hope, I discovered my purpose. The enthusiasm in this field originated not only from the technology, a mission to make every line of code matter.

Today, as I work on embedded systems. I am constantly reminded of my initial motivation. The desire to make a real impact with technology. Each project brings its own challenges, but with each line of code, each circuit design, I remember, I am part of something bigger. I am building systems that might one day save a life, secure a border, or guide an aircraft through a storm. Such a journey is worth every challenge, every late night, and every ounce of effort.

This vision keeps me moving forward, always ready to tackle the next challenge, knowing that even the smallest device can make a world of difference.

The Job Search

That stage of life, full of hope, energy, and a fair share of anxiety, is one most fresh graduates encounter. I had just completed my degree, armed with a solid understanding of electronics, programming, and a deep interest in embedded systems. I believed the job market would recognise my enthusiasm and promise. But soon enough, I learned reality proved more complex.

The Endless Applications

I started applying to every job listing that matched my skills. Each morning, I sat in front of my computer, tweaking my resume, crafting cover letters, and applying to companies that seemed like a perfect fit.

But weeks turned into months, and the only thing appearing in my inbox seemed to be a series of polite rejection emails. Some companies never responded at all. Others sent brief messages stating their search for more experienced candidates. It proved difficult to avoid taking it personally. I received no reply.

Time passed, and the rejections piled up. My friends and family kept trying to cheer me up, reminding me that finding the right job can take time. But I sensed I was falling behind. I would scroll through social media and encounter updates from my peers, people announcing new job offers, celebrating their first days at work, or posting photos of their new workspaces. And there I remained, still at home, still searching.

One evening, after another disheartening rejection, I sat down with my dad. He noticed my frustration. He did not offer empty reassurances but asked me a simple question: "Sateesh, why do you want to work in embedded systems?"

I thought about it for a while. It involved more than finding employment. I loved building and programming small devices, making them do something real, something tangible. Embedded systems are at the heart of every smart device. From medical instruments to satellites, the work I do can touch lives in invisible but powerful ways.

Embedded systems offer depth, specialisation, and relevance. I want to build products that are reliable, efficient, and meaningful, and embedded is the place for it.

A Moment of Doubt: Tears of Disappointment

After months of preparation and countless interviews, the phone rang, and a surge of hope washed over me. But as the HR representative began speaking, I sensed the familiar tone, the voice of yet another rejection. We appreciate your efforts, but at this time, we are unable to move forward with your application, she said.

I tried to muster a polite response, but the words did not make it out. With a weight pressing on my chest, my heart sank as I hung up the phone. The weight of my failures pressed down on me, and I could no longer hold back the tears. I sat there, staring at the empty wall, trying to grasp why I was not good enough, what I had done wrong.

The thought of facing my family with another piece of bad news was unbearable. Their sacrifices for my education and their dreams for me were clear to me. Reflecting on my father, I recalled his worn-out hands, tired smile, and the countless late nights he spent worrying about my future.

Overcome with emotion, tears flowed, each one carrying the weight of my fears and disappointments. It felt like everything I had worked for, everything I had hoped for, was slipping through my fingers. For a moment, I questioned whether I would ever find my place in this competitive world.

Turning Tears into Determination: A Challenge Accepted

The sting of rejection still echoed in my mind as I sat there, wiping away my tears. My chest ached with the weight of disappointment, but beneath that sadness, a new feeling surfaced, something stubborn and fierce.

I preoccupied my thoughts with my father's sacrifices.

After a deep breath, I stood and looked at myself in the mirror. Tears streaked my face, but my eyes now showed a resolve I had not seen in a long time. "Enough," I told myself. "It's time to turn this around."

To improve my skills, I grabbed my notebook and started listing everything I needed. Skills to sharpen, new programming languages to learn, and projects to take on. I confronted my weaknesses and transformed them into strengths. My focus on self-improvement was intended to better, strengthen, and prepare me for the next opportunity.

This time, it involved more than employment. Proving to myself that I could conquer difficulties. Converting every refusal into an incentive for greater dedication. The rejections were not walled anymore. They were stepping stones, pushing me forward.

As the night grew late, I found myself filled with a sense of purpose. I knew the challenge would be difficult, but I was prepared to face it. I would fight for the future I wanted, no matter how many rejections came my way. And when the next opportunity came, I would be ready to seize it.

The Struggle of Interviews

After what felt like an eternity, I got a call for an interview. It was a mid-sized tech firm that specialised in embedded systems. I spent days preparing for it, brushing up on my programming skills, and reading up on their recent projects.

Interview Day

On the day of the interview, I reached their office building half an hour early. After a few minutes in the waiting area, I was called in for the interview. Someone guided me into a conference room.

Interviewer: "Good morning, Sateesh." I see you are a recent graduate. So, what makes you think you are ready to jump into the world of embedded systems?"

"Good morning, Sir." My passion has always been in how software and hardware can come together to solve real-world problems. During my college days, I worked on several minor projects with microcontrollers. I may be a fresher, but I am eager to learn and tackle the challenges that come my way.

They asked me about memory management in C, real-time operating systems, and network protocols. I fumbled through some answers, and despite knowing the concepts, I just could not communicate my thoughts under pressure. The following day, I received a polite email stating, "Thank you for your time; however, we have moved forward with other candidates."

The Offer

A few days after the interview, I received an unexpected call. The HR person on the other end delivered the news with a tone that was both polite and firm. We have reviewed the feedback from your interview; she said. "While you show promise, we feel there are still areas in your technical skills that need further development. At this moment, we cannot consider you for the software developer role. However, if you are open to it, we would like to offer you a position as a Production Assistant."

A wave of disappointment washed over me, heavy and hard to ignore. It was not the outcome I had hoped for or the path I had envisioned for myself. But as I considered my situation, I realised I did not have numerous choices. So, swallowing my pride and pushing aside my initial sadness, I took a deep breath and accepted the offer. My situation was not ideal, but perhaps it would serve as a stepping stone to my intended destination.

A Journey from Production Assistant to Software Developer

It was not a straightforward path transitioning from being a production engineer to a software developer. The change required a shift not just in my skills but in the way I thought about problems, solutions, and the possibilities ahead. Looking back now, I see how each struggle became a stepping stone, pushing me closer to where I wanted to be.

The Early Days: Life on the Factory Floor

When I first started as a production engineer, the hum of machinery and the clank of metal against metal filled my days. My responsibilities included ensuring smooth production line operation, correct equipment calibration, and meeting output targets. It was a demanding job physically and mentally, but it gave me a solid foundation in problem-solving.

If a machine broke down in the middle of a shift, it was my job to figure out why. I had to solve problems in a stressful situation and get things working again. The role taught me discipline and a sense of responsibility, but there was always a nagging feeling that I wanted more.

The Daily Grind: A Journey of Sacrifice and Resilience

Every morning began the same way, long before the sun even considered rising. My alarm clock buzzed in the dark, and I forced myself out of bed, my legs heavy with the weight of exhaustion and worry. The thought of the miles I would travel that day felt like a burden before I even stepped out the door. My commute extended to a long journey, a two-hour bus ride into the city, squeezed between sleepy faces, all of us with the same weariness clinging to our expressions.

As I sat in my cramped seat, staring out at the passing lights, my mind drifted to my family and the difficulties we encountered. By the time I arrived at the office, the city's pulse quickened, and I forced myself to match its tempo. I pushed through each task with a determination that masked my fatigue. But sometimes in a quiet corner, alone, I would sense doubt beginning to take hold. Did this sacrifice truly have value? I doubted my ability to handle another day of this grind.

The ride home proved more difficult. Often, I would close my eyes, longing for sleep, but missing my stop remained unacceptable. To stay awake, I would press my fingers into my palms; a missed stop meant a longer walk back, further delaying rest.

My body ached from a long day, and I had just arrived home, yet unfinished tasks remained. My stomach growled, reminding me I had no one to prepare dinner. I needed to do it myself. Eating out was not an option; each rupee saved was a step closer to the dreams I was chasing. I began chopping vegetables in the dimly lit kitchen.

When dinner was ready, I needed to sit alone on the edge of my bed, the silence of the room pressing down on me. I ate slowly, appreciating the comforting taste of a homemade dish, despite its simplicity. The impression was that my only comfort stemmed from something I could manage, something I could keep. After eating, I would fall into bed, my body heavy with exhaustion, but my mind unable to stop spinning. I thought about my goals and the dreams that kept me moving forward.

I would whisper to myself in the dark, "One day, this will all be worth it. One day, you will make them proud."

And every morning when the alarm buzzed again, I found the strength to get up, to take that long ride, to cook for myself, and to face another day. A challenge, but this defined my reality.

I carried those sacrifices with me like a shield, a reminder of my objective. It was more than just survival; it was a promise to myself that I would not let my struggles define me. I would make it through, no matter how difficult each day seemed, because I knew deep down that there was a brighter future waiting for me, one bus ride, one meal, one day at a time.

Facing the Fire

It was just another afternoon at the office, the usual hum of work filling the air. My manager broke my immersion in my tasks when he called out, louder than usual. "Sateesh, in my office now!" The sternness in his tone made my heart skip a beat.

As I went to his cabin, I felt the weight of curious eyes on me. My mind raced. What might this concern? I knew I had made no mistake. But as soon as I stepped through the door, he was already on the attack.

He did not waste any time. "What's your intention? Are you trying to ruin everything?" he barked, his voice echoing through the room. "Do you have any idea how many problems your work has caused?"

I opened my mouth to respond, but he did not let me get a word in. He continued, his face turning redder by the second. "This is unacceptable, Sateesh! I will not tolerate this kind of incompetence. If you cannot shape up, I will throw you out of this company myself!"

I stood there stunned while he continued to unload, each word harsher than the last. I tried to make him understand I had double-checked everything, ensuring there was no mistake on my part. But his accusations drowned out my voice.

He ensured audibility for all. He left the door wide open, and his words hung in the air, turning every curious glance into a judgmental stare. My cheeks flushed with embarrassment. I sensed the weight of their gazes, the whispers that would inevitably follow. The humiliation cut deep.

When he finally stopped, it seemed an eternity had passed. He dismissed me with a wave of his hand, not even bothering to look me in the eye. "Get out of my sight," he muttered. "And think long and hard about whether you want to keep this job."

From his cabin, the sting of his words weighed heavily on each step for me. My colleagues rapidly looked away, pretending not to notice. The weight of it all pressed down on my shoulders as I sank back into my chair.

Anger, shame, and frustration swirled inside me. I understood it was not my error, yet I coped with his outburst. Part of me wanted to shout back, to defend myself. But I took a deep breath and steadied my mind.

I had a choice to make. I might let this moment break me, allow the embarrassment to linger, and eat away at my confidence. Or, I might use it as fuel, as a reason to work harder, to prove him and everyone else wrong. I decided on the latter.

Yes, I believed I had received unfair treatment. Yes, the sting of those words would not go away quickly. But I would not let this be the end of my story. I would change this situation, proving my resilience to my manager and myself.

A Turning Point: The Struggle Between Resignation and Responsibility

After that blistering confrontation with my manager, I sat at my desk, the anger and humiliation still fresh in my mind. The idea that persisted and grew louder became clear: I should quit.

Why should I stay in a place where they shouted at me, humiliated me in front of my peers, and treated me as insignificant? The notion of leaving through those glass doors for the last time was appealing — a sense of release from the pressure, from the persistent sense of not measuring up.

I pictured myself handing in my resignation, imagining the weight that might lift from my shoulders. I walk away with my pride intact, leaving behind this place where I felt unappreciated. But tempting as that idea was, a wave of reality crashed in.

Responsibilities. The word echoed in my mind, cutting through my frustration. The bills, rent, and student loans unpaid came to mind.

Walking away would have been simpler, but it lacked responsibility. I understood I needed to examine factors outside my own emotions.

Despite my immediate aversion, I had to acknowledge the persistent truth. If I left, I might struggle to get back on my feet, putting my family in a tougher situation than before. And deep down, I knew I could not let that happen.

So, I sat there, breathing deeply, trying to steady my thoughts. I forced myself to consider the wider context, to go beyond my damaged ego and wounded feelings. Slowly, I sensed the burning anger begin to cool, replaced by a steely resolve.

No, I will not quit. Not yet.

I would endure this, at least for now. I would find a way to rise above it, to use every challenge, every insult, as fuel to get better, to work smarter. This did not involve showing anything to my manager or my colleagues. It concerned showing something to myself. I was able to face the hard times and still find a way to progress.

It was possible a day would come when I would go by my decision, but not this one. Today, I would stay, and I would fight if not for me, then for those who had faith in me even when I doubted myself.

The Struggle: Balancing Work and Learning

Balancing my full-time job as a production assistant with learning to code was tough. I spent my days on the factory floor and my nights reading about programming, scripting, and Linux commands. I took online courses, watched tutorials, and worked on side projects, often staying up late into the night. It was exhausting, and there were many times I questioned whether I had made the right choice.

I remember struggling with debugging my code late at night. On some days, I experienced a lack of progress, trapped between two worlds—too technical to feel like a complete outsider in software but not skilled enough to enter the field.

The Breakthrough: Finding the Right Opportunity

I would occasionally cross paths with our software team, noticing the hurdles they faced in optimising certain processes. One day, I saw an opportunity to lend a hand. I worked after hours, diving into the issue they were grappling with. After some trial and error, I devised a solution that streamlined their workflow significantly.

The team found my solution impressive. My initiative did not go unnoticed. Soon after, I received heartfelt appreciation not just from the software team, but from my manager as well. Recognising my knack for problem-solving, he made a surprising and exciting decision: He immediately transferred me from the production department to the software team.

When Credit Goes Quiet

When I first joined the software team, I was eager to contribute and make an impact. My manager assigned me to develop a feature irrelevant to the current project. I understood the code required flawlessness, so I spent extra hours perfecting each line. But when I submitted my work, the team questioned it. Since I was still relatively new, they were unsure about trusting my code on such an important feature. My work went through multiple cross-checks, with each reviewer scrutinising it for any possible errors.

It was one of those weeks, late nights, cold coffee, and a bug that refused to die. I spent hours tracing logs, inspecting register values, and comparing memory dumps. Finally, after a long night alone at my desk, the missing piece clicked into place. A minor timing issue tucked deep within the ISR. I fixed it, tested it, and documented everything.

The next morning, I shared my findings with one of my colleagues whom I trusted, and I did not think much of it.

We all gathered around the whiteboard, and to my surprise, he stepped forward.

With confidence, he walked through the precise problem… the timing bug… the solution I dedicated the week to resolving. He spoke as if it was his discovery. No mention of me. Not even a glance.

The manager nodded, impressed.
"Well done. That was a tough one."
My eyes met his gaze for a second. He understood.
But I said nothing.

Not that I lacked courage. I just… did not want to turn a celebration into a confrontation.

Let him have this one, I thought. **Truth does not need applause. And recognition is not always loud.**

I walked back to my desk, opened my terminal, and got back to work. Because real engineers build more than just systems, they build **character**, too.

And deep inside, I understood:
The code knows who wrote it.
The log knows who stayed late.
And someday, the right people will also understand.

Turning Doubt into Trust: How Rigorous Review Transformed My Code and My Career

However, one challenge was that they did not allow me to touch the build system, considering it too complex and critical for a newcomer. At first, I experienced this restriction as a constraint. But rather than discouragement, I viewed it as a chance to show my capabilities.

Over the next few weeks, I began studying the build system in detail, learning its ins and outs, and noting every piece of its functionality. With persistence and a lot of late nights, I managed to develop a complete replica from scratch. My goal was not just to understand the system but to show that I could handle its complexity and add real value.

My presentation of the replica astonished my manager and team. No one had expected that I would handle such a huge job alone, and certainly not in only a month.

Their initial surprise soon turned into admiration. My initiative not only showed my technical skills but also built trust within the team. From that day on, I started working on the build system, and my software development career progressed significantly, ultimately enhancing my abilities and gaining team confidence.

Embracing the Next Challenge: Stepping into a New Role

After months of struggle, my persistence finally paid off. A startup valuing enthusiasm and willingness to learn over a traditional background invited me for an interview. They engaged in IoT solutions, something that combined my experience with production systems and my new passion for software development.

During the interview, I talked about my hands-on experience with automation on the factory floor, my understanding of hardware and sensors, and how I had been learning to write code to control them. They appreciated my unique perspective, seeing it as a strength rather than a limitation. I still recall the day my job offer arrived. That signified a moment of validation, a sign that the countless hours spent studying and coding had been worth it.

Beginning as a junior software developer felt like being thrown into the deep end, but I was eager to swim. Every day brought a challenge, yet it represented the challenge I had looked forward to. I brought the same problem-solving mindset from my days in production engineering, but applied it to writing code, creating software; it was efficient and reliable.

I found my background provided an advantage in comprehending hardware-software integration, making me a valuable team member bridging embedded systems and cloud services. My journey provided me with a unique viewpoint, and I learned to value it as a strength.

Looking Back: A Journey Worth Taking

When I look back, I see that the struggles I went through gave meaning to my journey. It was not simply a shift in professions; it was about proving my potential to myself. Even when rejections hurt and late nights made me doubt everything, I kept going. I had to trust in myself, even though it seemed others did not.

Today, I work as a software developer. I still use what I learned as a production engineer: hands-on problem-solving under pressure and a thorough understanding of systems. Those tough moments shaped me more than any classroom.

I learned patience, persistence, and how to continue when things appeared impossible. Those early days were full of struggle, but they also brought joy, the kind that comes from finally doing what you love.

That first job, those long nights, and the quiet victories became the foundation of who I am. Whenever I face something hard now, I remember where I started. And I am certain I will be okay.

Life was smooth for a while, same hours, same rhythm. But sometimes, the biggest changes come when we least expect them. One peaceful day transformed my understanding. Leading me down a previously unimaginable path… yet one I am profoundly thankful for.

CHAPTER 1

PLANTING A SEED TODAY IS THE PROMISE OF A BRIGHTER TOMORROW

Trust, Trials, and a New Beginning

It was a quiet Monday morning, after ten, when the message popped up:

"Sateesh, drop by my cabin. We need to discuss a new project."

My heart skipped half in anticipation, half in apprehension. I reached for my notepad, steadied my thoughts, and made my way down the corridor. *A new project?* The words echoed, brimming with possibility and pressure.

The boss was already staring at his screen when I stepped in. Without looking up, he gestured toward the chair across the table. I sat.

Afterwards, he spoke firm, precise.

We got the new requirements. They asked us to develop a prototype. Something light, modular, and running on embedded Linux. The device should talk to sensors, push data over a network, and have a simple front end, maybe Android or web, to display values.

He leaned back, locking eyes with me now.

"You will need to handle everything. OS bring-up, sensor integration, communication stack, and an app interface. And more importantly, build a team around it. You will not be alone, but you need to *own* it."

He paused. "You understand what's being asked?"

The room was quiet except for the low hum of the AC and the occasional flicker from the overhead lights. I sat across from my boss, notepad in hand, heart steady but alert.

He leaned back in his chair, eyes fixed on the whiteboard behind me. "Sateesh, this one's not going to be easy," he began. They gave us a core module, firmware-level work on new sensor boards, integration with an embedded OS, full-stack testing, and a live demo in six months. This is end-to-end. And it is ours.

You will need to coordinate with the hardware team, burn the bootloaders, get Linux running on the boards, and ensure communication protocols are solid—I2C, SPI, RS232, whatever it takes. And yes, build a web or app interface too. Have a wide-ranging perspective and consider the complete system.

I carefully recorded every word, fully aware that this assignment was more than a typical task it was a subtle evaluation of my leadership, my clarity, and my determination to succeed.

Sateesh, this one is different. You will need to build the team, drive the execution, and own the outcome. "Can you handle it?"

I nodded slowly, masking the swirl of doubt inside me. *Am I ready? Could I do this?*

I did not have all the answers. But one thing was obvious. I could not walk away from the opportunity to grow. I met his gaze, steady and sure. "I will not claim to be an expert, but I will learn, adapt, and give it my all. Yes, I can handle it."

He gave a small smile. Good. Come back once you have structured it. This is your battlefield now.

I need a plan within two days. Resources you need, timelines, and team structure. Think deeply.

As I stepped out of the cabin, the door clicked shut behind me, but the conversation echoed louder in my mind. This goes beyond simple code or delivery times. It is about ownership, trust, and leadership.

I walked back to my desk more slowly than usual. The familiar buzz of the office felt different now, like the backdrop of a stage I was about to step onto.

I sat down, opened my notebook, and wrote a single word on the blank page: "**Team**."

That is where I had to begin. Not with code or architecture diagrams, but with people.

And deep down, I understood: if I were going to lead this, I would have to become someone I had not been before.

Calling the Core: Forming My Dream Team

The project had become a reality. But it concerned more than myself; it involved the team I needed to select. In the quiet corner of the lab, I sat staring at the whiteboard—skills, strengths, weaknesses. Choosing the right team represented more than just strategy.

First stop—Nikita.

She occupied her regular corner, engrossed in a datasheet, with headphones partially covering her ears.

"Hey Nikita, got a minute?"

She pulled her headphones off. "Sure. What's up?"

I sat down next to her, lowering my voice with quiet intensity.

"We have got a new project—embedded systems, sensor interfacing, protocols, and application layers. It is going to test every bit of our skills. But I believe in you. You are the backbone of this team."

She looked at me, a determined glint in her eyes.

"I am ready. Let us make this happen."

Next—Akshay.

He remained at his desk, sketching a rough pin diagram on his notepad, deep in thought, lines crisscrossing like the logic in his mind.

"Akshay," I said, stepping closer with a smile. "How comfortable are you with microcontrollers?"

He glanced up, eyebrows raised. "Tough beasts," he replied. "But fascinating. Why?"

Because we have got a new project. And it revolves around them every heartbeat, every byte. It is no longer just theory. We will be building, debugging, and pushing limits.

His expression shifted, curiosity giving way to a spark of determination. "I'm in," he said. Time to make the datasheets proud.

Afterwards, Ashwin appeared.

He remained in the lab, attempting to make an LED flash on an evaluation board.

"Still fighting GPIOs?" I teased.

He smiled. "Learning curve. But I am getting there."

I handed him a sticky note with a project name. This will be your battlefield now. Embedded project. Real-time, low-level. Are you ready to go deeper?

He nodded slowly, eyes locking with mine. "Let's light more than LEDs this time."

Finally—Manasa.

She stayed in the pantry, sipping coffee and scrolling through something on her phone.

"Hey, Manasa," I said. "Up for a new challenge?"

She raised an eyebrow. "What kind?"

"One where you build the interface of an app, maybe a dashboard that speaks to an embedded system. Real-time data. Real users."

She paused, a smile creeping in. I have always wanted to work on something that talks to the real world. I am in.

By the end of the day, I had spoken to each of them. Not in a group meeting, but personally, individually. I sought to make clear to them their importance beyond a task list entry. They belonged to something meaningful.

A new journey had begun.

The Chosen Few: My Project Squad

A few days had slipped by since the project briefing. Amid restless nights, scattered notes, and hurried meals at my desk, I had assembled a team for their skills and for the grit I believed they had.

Now, it was time to present them formally.

I walked into the meeting room where my boss was waiting, arms folded, eyes sharp as ever. I took a breath and began.

"Sir, I've finalised the team for the embedded systems project,".

He gestured for me to continue.

"First, we have Nikita. She is our go-to expert with years of experience across embedded stacks, and she has always been the one to fall back on when things get tough."

He nodded, knowing Nikita's reputation well.

"Next, Akshay and Ashwin— both new to microcontrollers, but eager and fast learners. They are already brushing up on C and MCU architectures. I am confident with the right guidance, they will be ready."

I could see curiosity in his eyes now.

"Manasa will handle the Android application and possibly the web front-end. She is new to this domain but has a solid grasp of development."

He tilted his head slightly, still listening.

And I'll oversee the entire structure, technical ownership, communication between modules, and making sure we hit every milestone.

There was a moment of silence. He spoke next.

Good. I like that you have paired experienced minds with fresh energy. Remember, we build the best teams by pairing experience with potential. It may not be the safest route, but it is how growth happens. Remember this: people are observing. Make it count."

I nodded, already experiencing the weight but also the fire in those words.

Exiting the meeting room, I was no longer anxious.

I was ready.

Blueprint of the Journey

A calm Monday morning unfolded, the type where energy builds more gradually than coffee. I called for a quick sync-up, sensing it was the right moment to realign the team not with code, but with clarity.

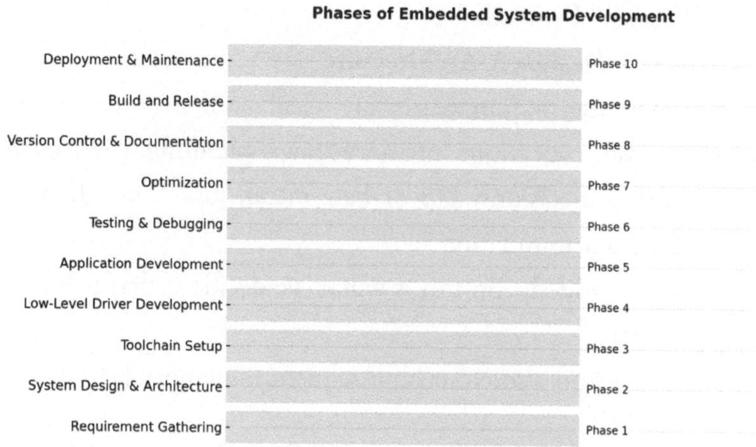

Everyone gathered around the whiteboard. Akshay twirled a marker in his fingers. Ashwin, Manasa and Nikita settled in with note apps ready.

I looked at them all, talented, motivated, and now hungry for the task we were about to start.

Before starting the project, let me walk you through the full life cycle of embedded development.

I drew a wide arc on the whiteboard and separated the arc into ten clear phases.

1. **Requirement Gathering**
   "Here is the start." We do not start by writing code; we start by asking questions. What does the product need to do? Who is using that? What are the constraints on power, cost, and performance?
   Akshay nodded. Are these user cases and hardware interfaces?

"Exactly," I smiled.

2. **System Design & Architecture**

   "Once the requirements are clear, we start designing. Processor selection, memory map planning, peripheral interface decisions, OS or bare-metal, task flow, all these define our foundation."

   Manasa added, "So this is where we decide if that is RTOS or Linux?"

   "Right. And also, your boot sequence, memory layout, and more."

3. **Toolchain Setup**

   "We cannot build without tools. This is where we bring in cross-compilers, linkers, debuggers, SDKs, everything that turns source into firmware."

   Ashwin chuckled. "And where half the team fights with environment paths."

   "Yup, and wins."

4. **Low-Level Driver Development**

   "Now we are closer to the silicon. GPIO, UART, I2C, SPI, ,ADC. This is where we talk to the hardware. One register at a time."

   Nikita raised an eyebrow. "Our favourite war zone."

   I laughed. "Exactly. That offers a more comprehensive learning experience than any tutorial.

5. **Application Development**

   "Once the drivers are stable, we move up protocol handling, logic control, UIs, if any. This is where the product looks like something useful."

6. **Testing & Debugging**
   "We simulate edge cases, run diagnostics, and stress test modules. Multimeters, CROs, analysers all come out now."
7. **Optimisation**
   Memory, CPU usage, and latency we optimize every aspect. Even if this succeeds, we will enhance it. That is an embedded mindset.
8. **Version Control & Documentation**
   "We commit with meaning. We document our designs, update READMEs, and maintain changelogs. Because a project without history is a headache waiting to happen."
9. **Build and Release**
   Automated scripts, reproducible builds, and release binaries, so even someone unfamiliar with the code's creation can install and execute the program.
10. **Deployment & Maintenance**
    This is when things get serious. This phase involves continuous field updates, post-deployment bug fixes, patching, and review of remote logs.

I capped the marker and looked at them.

A thoughtful, inspired quiet reigned.

The team said, "For the first time, we understand the bigger picture."

For the first time, everything became clear, we were not just coding anymore. We were building a system, phase by phase, with purpose.

Before You Dive In—Gear Up.

Chapter Summary

Chapter 1: Planting a seed today is the promise of a brighter tomorrow

Before we dive into building and debugging real systems, you need a solid base. Complete **Chapter 1** from the **Technical Notes** and get ready for what's ahead. Here's what to focus on:

- **What Are Embedded Systems?**
  Understand what makes an embedded system different from a general-purpose system, why size, speed, and reliability matter, and where these systems power our world, from medical devices to aerospace.

- **Development Cycle of Embedded Systems**
  Learn the complete lifecycle—from **requirement gathering → system design → coding → testing → optimisation → deployment, and maintenance**. This is the blueprint for everything you will do in this book and in your career.

Action Step:

Review **Chapter 1** thoroughly. Understand why embedded systems exist, how to build them, and the steps involved in bringing an idea to life. This foundation will make every upcoming chapter easier to grasp.

CHAPTER 2

BUILDING THE CORE SKILLS - WHAT MATTERS MOST

Igniting the Spark

It was one of those quiet mornings when the sun filtered softly through the blinds, and the aroma of filtered coffee still lingered in the lab. I stood by the whiteboard, staring at a blank slate, not with uncertainty but with anticipation.

The room slowly filled, Nikita took her usual corner seat, Akshay and Ashwin followed, slightly bleary-eyed, while Manasa walked in with a notepad in hand, already scribbling something.

I looked at each of them, then smiled.

"Team, before we build great things, we must first build ourselves."

They looked up.

We have got a powerful journey ahead, microcontrollers to tame, sensors to control, and boards to bring alive. But before the hands-on magic begins, there is something else we need: **mastery of the foundation**.

Nikita raised her eyebrow. "You mean like C?"

"Not only **C**," I nodded. **C programming** is our sword it is how we speak to the hardware, how we write drivers, and how we debug what others cannot see. It is not just a language; it is the **heartbeat of embedded systems**.

I turned to the whiteboard and began writing:

- **C Programming**
- **Microcontrollers & Architectures**

- **RTOS Concepts**
- **Communication Protocols – I2C, SPI, UART, RS232**

"These," I said, pointing at the list, "are the tools that will carry us through. We can only blink LEDs if we do not understand RTOS task scheduling and how interrupts affect operations. But with them, we will be building systems that breathe, respond, and scale."

Akshay looked thoughtful. "It sounds... intense."

Yes, it is, but it is also exciting. This is your opportunity to execute a project and to transform as engineers.

Ashwin chimed in, "So… how do we start?"

Simple. We split. Each of you will explore and teach one topic back to the group every week. We will study together, break things, fix them, and learn from each other.

There was a long pause, followed by a few nods.

Manasa smiled. "I always wanted to understand how I2C actually works."

I responded, "Let us investigate not only to fulfil deadlines but to create something we can be proud of. Something that carries a part of each one of us."

And that morning, something shifted. Not in the code or the hardware, but in the minds of the team. The fire had been lit.

Beginning: Mastery begins with these initial steps.

By the next day, the team displayed their in-depth study of the system on the whiteboard as diagrams, notes, and a growing list of tasks. A change in the room's energy was perceptible. There was a quiet buzz of determination, like a group preparing not only for a project, but for something bigger, something personal.

I walked in with a stack of printed datasheets and reference manuals. "Alright, team," I said, placing them on the table. "Let's build our war room."

Each member stood near their topic on the whiteboard:

Akshay, the most hands-on among us, had picked **Microcontrollers**.

"I'm going to understand every pin, every register," he said, flipping through the datasheet like a novel. And by next week, I will explain how GPIOs, timers, and ADCs work in real-time.

Ashwin, slightly hesitant at first, had chosen **C Programming**.

I want to exceed simple code writing, he said. I want to understand pointers, memory management, and interrupt routines. It is scary, but I will get there.

Manasa surprised us by picking **Communication Protocols**.

"I2C, SPI, RS232, I have used libraries, but never really understood them. I want to learn what goes on behind those APIs."

Nikita, ever the all-rounder, volunteered for **RTOS Concepts**.

"Multitasking, scheduling, mutexes, I'll break it down into examples we can all simulate on our dev boards."

I stood back, proud.

This is more than skill-building, I reminded them. It is team building. When each of you understands these pillars, we will build faster, debug smarter, and solve deeper problems.

Afterwards, we created a simple plan: a focused session every Thursday afternoon, an hour for teaching, Q&A, and practical demonstrations. No slides. Only whiteboard, code, and curiosity.

On that Thursday, Akshay led the first session.

With a small dev board plugged into his laptop, he walked us through blinking an LED using direct register manipulation. No libraries. No shortcuts.

"See this bit?" he said, pointing at the ODR register. Toggling this changes the output voltage on the pin. That is how it blinks.

Ashwin whispered, "This is the first time I'm actually seeing what's under digitalWrite."

We all clapped at the end. It was not perfect, but it was raw, real learning. The kind that sticks.

By the end of the day, the whiteboard had a new quote, written in Manasa's tidy handwriting:

"Learn it, then build it."

And we were just getting started.

From Learning to Building

A few weeks in, the Thursday sessions had become the heartbeat of our team. The meetings were not just about the technical details anymore; they involved discussions, disagreements, debates, and breakthroughs. Each session concluded with a similar impression: improvement was evident.

Now, it was **Ashwin's** turn.

He stood at the whiteboard, a bit nervous, holding a marker in one hand and a printout of some C code in the other.

"Okay," he began, I spent last week rewriting the LED toggle code without using global variables. Following that, I explored pointers extensively.

There was a mix of nods and raised eyebrows.

Ashwin drew a simple diagram: memory addresses, pointer variables, and how they relate to hardware registers in embedded programming.

When you pass a pointer to a function, you are giving direct memory access. That is how we modify register values for peripherals.

He connected it back to Akshay's earlier GPIO example, this time writing it in a cleaner, modular format.

I could see the shift not only in Ashwin's explanation, but in his acceptance of it.

"Beautiful work," I said. "And it's going to help when we start abstracting hardware logic into reusable drivers."

By now, the lines between learning and doing were fading.

During that week's sprint, **Manasa** had to interface a sensor using I2C. It did not work the first time. Or the second.

But she remembered her studies from the previous week and shared: clock stretching, ACK/NACK bits, and timing constraints.

"Hold on," she said. The slave is not acknowledging after the address byte. Either it is not wired properly, or the address is wrong.

Ten minutes later, it worked. And she smiled.

Meanwhile, **Nikita** had taken her RTOS learnings into code. She built a simple FreeRTOS setup on our dev board with three tasks blinking LEDs at different intervals.

This is how we will later separate sensor reading, data processing, and communication tasks in our real firmware, she explained.

"It seems we're actually getting project-ready," Akshay said, half-joking, but I knew he meant it.

By the end of the month, our daily standups had gone beyond what we did. They were about what we learned, and how that learning was unlocking real progress.

I looked around and thought:

This is not just a team anymore.

This is a crew.

A group of self-driven, sharp minds getting ready to take on something real, something big.

And for the first time in a while, I experienced this… certainty.

We are going to build something great.

The Design Review Room

The conference room was unusually quiet for a Monday morning. Across the table, I spread my design diagrams, block diagrams, timing charts, and flowcharts that I had refined over weeks of late nights.

My boss entered with a stack of notes, placed them gently on the table, and looked at me with a half-smile.

"Alright, walk me through it," he said.

I began outlining the system:

- **Hardware Abstraction Layer** to keep the drivers modular.
- **Interrupt-driven I/O** to reduce CPU load.
- **Watchdog timers** for safety in case of hangs.
- **Configurable build profiles** for debug and production modes.

As I spoke, he leaned in, occasionally tapping his pen on certain sections of the diagram.

"Why did you choose this communication protocol instead of the faster alternative?"

"What happens if the sensor fails mid-operation?"

"How will this scale if we add two more modules next year?"

Each question cut deeper into the design, forcing me to think beyond what was on paper. I explained my reasoning sometimes confidently, sometimes searching for the right answer.

At one point, he paused, then said:

"You have built a good plan, but remember, a design is only as strong as its weakest assumption. Question everything, even your own choices."

By the end of the review, red annotations and sticky notes covered my diagrams. It was not easy seeing my neat design dissected like that, but I walked out with a stronger blueprint than I had walked in with.

That day taught me a lesson: design reviews are not about proving you are right; they are about finding the blind spots before they cost you in the field.

Foundations of Trust: Presenting My Team

The door clicked shut behind me as I stepped into the boss's cabin. Sunlight streamed through the blinds, casting stripes across his desk.

"Alright, Sateesh," he said, glancing up from his notepad, "you said you're ready with the team. Let's hear it."

"Before I begin," I said, "I'd like to introduce you to the team."

One by one, they stepped in.

Nikita stood first — confident, composed.

"She has been the backbone of our architecture planning and RTOS integration. When the system needs clarity, she brings it."

The boss gave a small nod.

Akshay followed — a spark in his eyes.

"He came in new to embedded systems, but today he is debugging with confidence and writing clean drivers. He has become our go-to for hands-on microcontroller work."

Ashwin arrived next, more reserved, yet equally resolute.

"He has worked hard to master low-level C, focusing on clean, maintainable code.

Manasa stepped forward last.

"She started with no background in Android or web, but now she is building test interfaces and exploring data visualisation for our sensor output. She is growing fast and eager."

I looked at all of them. Next: Following that, at the boss's.

As a team, we have not only strengthened our technical foundation. We have built real modules. GPIO control, UART-based sensor communications, and a basic RTOS task structure.

The boss leaned back in his chair, looking at each face.

"Hmm. Looks like a young crew, but a solid one."

There was a pause. He smiled—a seldom-seen smile.

"Good work, Sateesh. Let us see how far this team can go."

I stepped back, not only with relief but also with pride. This was our team. And this… was only the beginning.

Cafeteria Chronicles: Where the Real Debugging Happens

Friday afternoon arrived, the air heavy with strong filter coffee and distant clattering steel plates. We had finished a long debugging session, and I suggested we take a break. The team needed it not only to rest but also to laugh. And there is no better place for that than our good old cafeteria.

We found our usual corner table scratched, unsteady, but full of memories. Plates of samosas arrived, and the jokes began even before the chutney's arrival.

Nikita started the swing. If Akshay's LED blink took that long, we would have weekly daylight savings.

Akshay, pretending to be wounded, grabbed his chest. I gave it a personality. Not all LEDs are required to blink like robots.

Ashwin, always the quiet sniper, chimed in, "Yeah, but yours blinked once... and died. I thought you invented a new Morse code."

The table roared with laughter.

By now, we all laughed heartily. Even Abhishek and Jayalaxmi, who had recently joined the table, got pulled into the madness.

Jayalaxmi and Abhishek may be on a different team, but they have always been easy to contact. Trusted friends and quiet problem-solvers, they step in whenever we hit a wall.

No samosas remained; the laughter echoed, and for a moment, we were not engineers or developers, or team leads. We were just a group of friends, interacting and building something beyond a simple project companionship.

Leaving the cafeteria, we felt both well-fed and energised.

Sometimes, the best debugging happens over a cup of chai and a well-timed roast.

Chapter Summary

Chapter 2: Building the Core Skills – What Matters Most

This chapter is not only about learning topics; it is about developing your mindset as an engineer who thinks in bits, timing, and control.

Topics to Complete in Chapter 2:

- **C Programming**
  Master the language of embedded systems—pointers, memory, bitwise operations, and control logic.
- **Microcontroller vs. Microprocessor**
  Understand the architecture, differences, and where each fits in real-world applications.

- **RTOS Concepts**
  Discover the heartbeat of real-time systems—tasks, scheduling, context switching, and determinism.
- **Communication Protocols: I2C, SPI, UART, RS232**
  Learn how devices talk to each other—synchronously and asynchronously.

Why This Chapter Matters:

Because everything that follows drivers, hardware debugging, performance tuning, and deployment relies on these fundamentals.

Complete **Chapter 2** with **focus and intent.**

Do not merely read code, experiment, break things, and fix them.

CHAPTER 3

DIVE INTO LINUX AND LEARN THE FREEDOM OF SHAPING YOUR OWN SYSTEM

Unlocking the World of Linux

It was following lunch. The cafeteria jokes still lingered in our smiles, but I could sense a hunger in the room not for food, but for understanding. The kind of hunger I would once feel, sitting on cold plastic chairs in my early days, staring at terminals with more questions than answers.

I clapped my hands.

"Alright, team. It is my turn now."

The room quieted down.

Everyone gathered, **Nikita** leaned forward with her pen ready, and **Akshay** and **Ashwin** brought their laptops, screens glowing. **Manasa**, curious as ever, sat up straight. The whiteboard stood tall behind me, like a canvas waiting to be painted.

"I know you've all been diving into microcontrollers, sensors, and communication protocols. But today, let us zoom out. Let us talk about the ground we stand on."

A few eyebrows raised. Interest sparked.

I wrote one word on the board: **Linux**.

"Alright team," I began, "before we go further into embedded systems, there is something you all must truly understand: **Linux**. Without it, we are just scratching the surface. With it, we can build worlds."

Akshay frowned. "But isn't Linux just another operating system? Like Windows?"

I smiled. "That is the mistake most make. Linux is not just an operating system; it is the foundation on which almost every embedded platform is built. Think routers, IoT devices, drones, and even satellites. Linux is the silent heartbeat inside them."

Nikita leaned in, curious. "So where do we start?"

"Start with the basics," I said, opening a terminal on the projector screen.

- **The Shell**: "This black window? It is your laboratory. Commands are your experiments."
- **Filesystems**: Imagine it like a library. The system arranges everything, organising it under folders such as /bin, /usr, and /home. Each file, each directory, has a purpose. "Everything in Linux is a file: your keyboard, your USB drive, even processes. Understand that, and you will never be lost."
- **Permissions**: "The system is secure because not everyone can touch everything. Learn chmod, chown, and you control access like a gatekeeper."
- **Processes**: "Type ps or top, and you will see the veins of the system pumping. This is how Linux lives, breathes, and multitasks."

Ashwin chuckled. "Feels like learning a new language."

"Exactly," I replied. "Linux is the language of engineers. You cannot master embedded systems without speaking it fluently. And once you do, you will not just run commands, you will understand *why* the system behaves the way it does."

Manasa asked softly, “And what happens once we master it?”

I leaned back, smiling. “Then you stop being just programmers. You become system engineers, the ones who do not just write code but understand the stage at which the code performs. That is the difference between a developer and an embedded engineer.”

The room fell silent, but it was the good kind of silence, the kind that meant curiosity had been sparked. I saw the gleam in their eyes. They were not just learning Linux; they were stepping into a whole new world.

Let us talk about **process management**. When your code runs, it becomes a process. It is like giving life to instructions.”

Processes are born, they run, they exit. But sometimes, they misbehave, consume memory, hang, or spawn children that never stop. Understanding their control is vital.

The room was silent, focused.

I looked around.

Today, I am more than your teammate. I am your guide. Everything I learned the hard way, I will show you the smarter way. This involves more than simply making a product. It is about becoming engineers who **understand what is really happening under the hood**.

A pause. A smile followed.

“Alright. Fire up your terminals. Let us begin.”

Terminal Time and the Engineer's Quiz

The team quickly gathered around, opening their terminals like soldiers unsheathing their swords. The familiar black screens filled with blinking cursors stared back, eager for commands.

"Okay," I said, walking behind them. "Let us start simple. Type: ls -l."

They did. A list appeared, some in blue, some in green, some in white, with columns of strange letters and numbers.

"Let's decode that," This is more than output. It is a story. The first column shows file permissions. Remember those rwx flags we talked about? This tells you who can do what with each file.

Nikita leaned in, murmuring, "So if I see drwxr-xr-x, that's a directory where I can read, write, and execute, but others can only read and execute?"

"Absolutely!" I grinned. "You're catching on."

"Now try this," "Create a new file: touch test.txt. Afterwards, run ls -l again."

They all followed along, the little "aha" moments twinkling in their eyes.

Akshay, curious as ever, asked, "What if I want to make it read-only for everyone?"

Try "**chmod 444 test.txt**", I suggested. Next, open it and try editing. The system will not let you because permissions speak louder than intentions.

Laughter bubbled up from Manasa. "This feels like magic."

"This is only the start," I said. "Let us switch gears. Ever wondered what happens when you run a program?"

I approached the whiteboard and sketched the process life cycle: created (fork) → running (exec) → terminated (exit).

"Alright… let's have some fun," I said with a smirk.

The board: The board is clear.

"Pop Quiz Time!"

Groans and chuckles broke out.

"I'll ask, and whoever gets it right, wins… a coffee from me tomorrow!"

The room went quiet. Stakes were high.

Question 1: "What command shows all running processes with a tree-like hierarchy?"

Ashwin's hand shot up. "pstree?"

"Correct! One coffee on the board."

Question 2: "Which command traces all system calls made by a process?"

"strace!" Akshay blurted.

"Fast and right! You are on fire."

Question 3: "What's the difference between > and >> in command-line redirection?"

Nikita raised her hand. "> overwrites, >> appends."

"Perfect. You are all earning your Linux stripes today."

They laughed and celebrated each answer like mini victories.

I leaned on the table and looked at them with pride. "See? It is not about memorising commands. It is about understanding the why and how behind them. That is what makes an embedded engineer powerful."

We wrapped up the session as the clock neared evening.

But something in the atmosphere had changed not only knowledge but also confidence. They were more than just team members. They were builders, thinkers, doers.

To the Builders of Tomorrow: It is Time to Go Deeper

If you have made it this far, congratulations. But the real magic lies ahead.

Now's the time to complete **Chapter 3** of my **Technical Notes.** This chapter is the bridge between being a developer and becoming a true systems engineer.

Chapter Summary

Chapter 3: Dive into Linux and learn the freedom of shaping your own system

Here is what you will master next:

- **What is Linux?** Understand its philosophy, power, and purpose.
- **What is Shell & Basic Linux Commands**
  Get comfortable with the shell, it is your gateway to controlling the system. Master the essential commands for navigation, file operations, and process handling.

- **Filesystem & File Permissions** – Know what controls access and security.
- **Program Execution in Linux** – What really happens when you type ./a.out.
- **Linux Process Management** – Learn how tasks are born, managed, and terminated.

Complete **chapter 3.** Absorb every detail. Practice relentlessly.

Because what comes next will demand not just knowledge but mastery.

Let us get ready for the real challenges.

CHAPTER 4

THE SOUL OF LINUX LIES IN KNOWING HOW IT WORKS BENEATH THE SURFACE

Let Me Tell You How Linux Wakes Up

It was one of those crisp mornings where the sun perfectly hit the lab windows, making even the debug logs appear poetic. The team settled in the lab with hot coffee, powered on the boards.

Ashwin, eyes glued to the serial console, asked, *"Sateesh, what exactly happens when we power on this board? I see logs flying, but I cannot follow anything."*

Akshay nodded. "Yeah, the screen lights up, the kernel prints a bunch of stuff, and afterwards, the shell pops up. It is like magic.

I smiled, stood up, and walked toward the whiteboard. *"Alright, team, let's decode the magic."*

I drew a simple flow:

1. **Power On → Boot ROM**
2. **Bootloader (U-Boot)**
3. **Kernel Load**
4. **Init System (systemd or init)**
5. **User Space Begins**

"Let me break this down," I said, grabbing a marker.

Power On / Reset:

"When the board is powered up, the processor does not know anything. So, it looks for instructions in a small internal Boot ROM. That is the hard-wired starting point."

Bootloader:

"Next, the Boot ROM hands control to the bootloader like U-Boot. Think of this as an early-stage planner. It initialises RAM, identifies storage devices, and loads the Linux kernel image into memory."

Ashwin whispered, "So U-Boot is like BIOS in PCs?"

"Exactly," I nodded. "It's our embedded BIOS."

Kernel Boot:

"Once the kernel is loaded, it takes over. It sets up memory, initialises drivers, mounts the root filesystem, and starts the first process, usually 'init' or 'systemd'."

Init System:

"This is where the OS starts feeling like a system. It brings up services, network, logging, and user interfaces, all driven by configuration."

User Space:

"And finally, you get the login shell, or your application starts running. Now Linux is alive."

Manasa scribbled in her notebook. "So that's why our UART shows garbage if U-Boot did not set the clock?"

"Yes. Every stage relies on the previous one doing its job right."

Akshay smiled. "I used to think Linux just… appeared."

Now you understand, I grinned. "Linux does not just boot. It *wakes up*, stage by stage. And if anything in between fails, you do not get a system."

The room was silent for a moment, silent with the sound of gears turning.

Nikita chuckled, "Nice breakdown, Sateesh. But next time, I expect a full animated movie popcorn included!"

We all laughed.

Peeking Beneath the Hood: Our Journey into Kernel Internals

The week held much excitement and stress. The air in the lab buzzed not with noise but with curiosity.

It all started when Akshay glanced up from his terminal one afternoon and asked, "Sateesh, we know how Linux boots and handles user programs, but… what really goes on beneath? Inside the kernel?"

I smiled. It was a question I had waited for.

"That's where the real magic lies," "Let's go deeper."

We cleared off the whiteboard. I picked up a marker and began drawing what looked like layers of an onion.

"Think of the kernel as the heart of the OS. It is what talks to hardware, manages memory, schedules processes, handles system calls, and much more. It is the bridge between your application and the bare metal beneath."

Nikita, always sharp, chimed in, "Is that where context switching happens?"

"Definitely!" I nodded. "Let's break it down."

We spent the next hour talking about:

- **Process Management** – How the kernel juggles hundreds of processes, giving each a slice of CPU time.
- **Memory Management** – Page tables, virtual addresses, and how the kernel makes sure no process steps into another's memory.
- **System Calls** – How user-space programs politely knock on the kernel's door using calls like read(), write(), and fork().
- **Interrupt Handling** – How the kernel drops everything to respond to hardware signals and then gracefully resumes its tasks.
- **Kernel Modules** – little pieces of code we could write ourselves and plug directly into the running kernel.

Ashwin looked stunned. "So… we can actually write code that runs inside the OS?"

"You can," I said. "Carefully."

I gave them a simple sample module, hello_world.c, which prints a message upon loading and another upon removal.

We compiled it using make; afterwards, we ran insmod.

"Check dmesg," I said.

Their eyes lit up as they saw:

[info] Hello, kernel! Module loaded.

Ashwin laughed. “We just *spoke* to the kernel!”

“Yes,” I said. “And from here on, it listens.”

The rest of the day flew by. We explored **/proc**, discussed kernel threads, and how scheduling policies like SCHED_FIFO or SCHED_RR shaped system behaviour. They began viewing Linux as more than an operating system, a vibrant, responsive machine under their control.

As the sun dipped below the horizon, our lab still buzzed with the quiet confidence of a team transformed. From filesystem fundamentals to process management, from boot flow to permissions. We had peeled back the layers of Linux together. What once felt daunting now sparked curiosity. The team was not just following commands anymore; they were speaking Linux like a native tongue.

“At this level, the distinction is clear: a developer makes the system work; an embedded engineer understands why it works, how it breathes, and what makes it tick.”

With that, I looked around and smiled. Alright, team, let us call it a day. You have earned it.

Chapter Summary

Next Stop: Chapter 4: The soul of Linux lies in knowing how it works beneath the surface

Before diving deeper into system programming, make sure you have completed **Chapter 4** from the **Technical Notes**. This chapter forms the backbone of everything you will build next. Here is what to focus on:

- **How Linux Boots**
  Understand the entire journey from powering on the board to reaching the user space. Grasp how bootloaders, the kernel, and init systems work together.
- **Kernel Modules**
  Learn how modules extend kernel functionality without rebooting the system. Know the difference between static and loadable modules and why they matter.
- **Kernel Internals Study**
  Peek under the hood, process scheduling, memory management, interrupts, and system calls. This understanding separates a developer from a true embedded engineer.

Complete **Chapter 4** of my technical notes. Run the commands, insert and remove a module, and explore **/proc**. These concepts are the foundation for **everything that comes next in embedded Linux development**.

CHAPTER 5

POWER, PRECISION & PREPAREDNESS

Before the Boards Arrive

The past few weeks have been a whirlwind of learning. From understanding Linux internals to building our first kernel modules and diving into device drivers. Our team had grown in knowledge, skill, and confidence.

One afternoon, we were all gathered in the lab, discussing pointers and quirks of /proc, when Ashwin looked up and said with a grin, "Guys, we have learned a lot! But when are those new boards arriving? I am getting restless."

Akshay chimed in, "Yeah! All this learning must meet some hardware now."

Nikita smiled. "They said it will ship this week." But before we dive into more kernel panics and driver bugs… how about a break?

I looked around at their faces, tired but glowing with pride. They deserved a breather.

"All right," "let's talk to the boss." If he agrees, we will plan a short team outing, some fresh air, fun, and food before we get back into serious board-level debugging.

The Walk to the Cabin

Later that afternoon, I walked up to the boss's cabin and knocked gently.

"Come in," he said, glancing up from his screen.

I stepped inside with a smile. "Sir, I only needed a minute."

He leaned back. "Go ahead, Sateesh."

I wanted to give a quick update. The team has really picked up the pace, Linux, drivers and embedded basics. We have covered a lot. The team's excitement is building for the upcoming boards, but I thought maybe, before we jump into the next grind, we should take a short team outing. Only one day. A break before the boards arrive.

He looked thoughtful. "You're saying they've earned it?"

I nodded. "More than that. They have built a bond. This break, in my opinion, will only make them stronger.

He smiled faintly. Alright. One day. Please address safety concerns and keep me informed.

"Yes, sir. Thank you."

Back in the Lab

When I returned, the team was waiting.

"So?!" Manasa asked.

I gave a slow nod and said, "Pack your bags. The boss said yes."

Cheers erupted. Abhishek and Jayalaxmi, always the cheerful allies from the other team, joined us for the outing. With their arrival, the fun doubled, and the laughter only got louder.

As laughter echoed through the lab, I realised something. We were not just a group of engineers anymore. We were growing into something stronger: a true team, bound by trust, learning, and shared purpose.

The boards would arrive soon. The real challenge was yet to begin. But for now, it was time to celebrate how far we had come.

Out of Office: Team Mode On!

The sun rose a little brighter that Saturday. There was no code to debug, no boot logs to scroll through, and no command lines blinking back at us. Today, we were not engineers; we remained just a group of colleagues enjoying a deserved rest.

We all met near the office gate, backpacks slung over our shoulders and laughter already bubbling. Jayalaxmi arrived with homemade snacks. Akshay and Ashwin remained busy taking selfies. and Nikita, as usual, double-checked whether we had sunscreen.

Where is Manasa? I asked, looking around.

"Running late," Abhishek replied. "But she said she'll catch us at the highway stop."

I exchanged a nod, we are ready.

The Journey

The cab swerved through winding roads as music played, and voices rose in half-sung lyrics and full-blown laughter. We played dumb charades, shared funny office incidents, and pulled each other's legs relentlessly.

Ashwin mimicked the boss, said, "You have only 5 minutes. Convince me!" and everyone burst into laughter.

"Guys, do you remember the day we all burnt the sensor boards?" Akshay joked.

"I'll never forget," I laughed. "The smell of toasted PCB still haunts me!"

At Resort

The resort welcomed us with open skies and open hearts. We had dived into the lazy pool, played volleyball, tried and failed at archery, and laughed until our stomachs hurt.

During lunch under a shady mango tree, we sat together, plates full and hearts fuller.

"I needed this break," said Manasa, taking a sip of juice. "We have worked hard. But this… this makes it worth it."

I looked at each of them and how far we had come since that day I hesitated to lead. From hesitant engineers to a team that could joke, fail, learn, and rise together.

The sun began to set, and with it, the outing drew to a close. But we were returning with lighter hearts and stronger bonds.

Back to Work Soon…

As the cab pulled back toward the city lights, I looked out the window with a smile.

The boards would arrive next week. Challenges would follow.

I did not have all the answers, but I had something better: a team that believed. And together, that was enough to face anything.

The boards have arrived!

It was a regular weekday morning, keyboards clicking, coffee brewing, and the quiet hum of our office floor. I was about to check my emails when a knock came at the door.

"Parcel for the development team," said the receptionist.

I walked over, signed the receipt, and there they were, **our development boards**, neatly packed and shimmering with promise.

I carried the box like a treasure chest back to our bay.

"Guys," I called out, trying to keep a straight face. "You might want to take a look at this."

"What's that?" Ashwin asked.

I did not answer. I placed it on the table. A sharp click as the flaps popped open.

Akshay peeked over his monitor. "Is that what I think it is?"

"Yep," I said, grinning. "The wait is over."

Excitement Unboxed

Everyone gathered around as I carefully cut the seal. Nikita had already begun reviewing the part numbers. Ashwin found the datasheets, and Manasa readied her camera to film the unboxing like a festive event.

"Look at this Sensor," said Abhishek. "This is more positive than our expectations!"

Jayalaxmi, always the silent observer, simply smiled and nodded, ready to dig into debugging once things got rolling.

We laid them out on the table, carefully labelled each one, and started dividing responsibilities.

"This is the moment we've been building toward," I said. "Every lesson, every late night, every setback, it all led us here. Now, let us put our knowledge to the test."

The team already started discussing test points, GPIOs, pin mappings, and voltage tolerances. Nikita was reviewing firmware hooks, while Manasa sought sample data formats to contemplate the frontend.

I stepped back for a moment, taking it all in.

The boards arrived; in addition, the team was ready.

The Debug Lab Diaries: Demystifying Multimeters, CROs, and Analysers

We all stood around the bench, the new board resting like a sleeping beast under the lab lights.

Excitement crackled in the air. I lifted a hand, steady and firm, halting the rush to power on.

"Not yet," I said.

The team looked at me, curious, eager.

"Power comes last," I reminded them. "First, we verify because good engineering begins with respect for the hardware."

I pointed to the board.

"First visual inspection. Look for bent pins, missing components, and bad solder joints. Trust your eyes first."

The First Measurement

Freshly unboxed and with pins untouched, the board waited on the bench to breathe its first signal. Eyes flicking between datasheets and doubt, the team stood around with cables coiled in their hands.

"Alright, before anything else..." I said, holding up a tool that looked deceptively simple, "Let's meet your new best friend, **the multimeter.**"

Akshay raised an eyebrow. That thing? I believed it was only for examining battery levels.

I smiled. "That 'thing' can save your board and your day."

I placed it gently on the table and clicked it on.

"This," I said, pointing to the dial, "is DC voltage mode. And this is continuity. Get familiar with that beep; it is the sound of no short circuits."

Ashwin leaned closer. "So... we check every pin?"

"Not every," I replied. Only the correct ones. GND to VCC no shorts. Afterwards, inspect your regulators and verify your supply lines. Wait for the all-clear before starting.

Nikita took it next, testing a capacitor with the assurance of someone discovering a secret language. "It beeped," she said. "That's good, right?"

"Excellent," I nodded. "That beep is your first defence against fried silicon."

Manasa, notebook in hand, scribbled diagrams with the precision of a cartographer. "I like this. It is like checking a pulse before surgery."

I stepped back and observed as they passed the multimeter around like a ceremonial object, probing, measuring, verifying.

The device was still off. But the team? They were switched on.

Before you can blink an LED or run a sensor…

You learn to listen to the silence between the circuits.

Signals in Silence: Learning to See the Invisible

The board had powered on and flashed our firmware. LEDs blinked. Serial logs scrolled. But something was... off.

"The sensor's not responding," Akshay muttered, peering at the I^2C init line in the code.

"We're sending the signal," Manasa added, but getting no ACK. It is like shouting into the void.

I saw the perplexed expressions around the lab bench and then moved toward the cabinet to retrieve a dusty, mysterious piece of equipment.

Alright, team, I said, placing the device down with a thud, "time to meet the eyes and ears of an embedded engineer, **the CRO and Logic Analyser.**"

Nikita tilted her head. "That thing with the wave squiggles?"

I smiled. Precisely. A CRO does not lie. It shows you the raw pulse of your hardware, the truth behind every failed communication, every stubborn bug.

I connected the probes, grounding one, clipping the other to the SDA line.

"Watch," I said, as I hit the trigger.

Suddenly, the screen came alive, waves dancing in perfect rhythm.

"Whoa," Ashwin whispered. "Is that… the signal?"

That, I nodded, is the board speaking. Now, let us find out why no one is listening.

Following this, I slid over to the Logic Analyser. "And this one decodes the language for you. SPI, I^2C, UART, whatever protocols on the wire, this translates it to human."

Manasa leaned in. Thus, our activities extend beyond coding. We… spy on the signals?

"Not a spy," I said with a chuckle. Observe, decode, and understand. This is where embedded engineering gets poetic, **reading the silence between bits.**

We connected the logic analyser to the I^2C lines, opened the decoder tool, and ran a capture. One glance and there it was: a timing glitch right before the ACK.

"Clock stretched too long," Nikita said. That's why the sensor dropped out.

Akshay whistled. And we would not have found that using only logs.

"Truly," "Code shows intent. But these tools show reality."

That evening, the lab lights dimmed, but the screen kept pulsing, telling stories in voltage and time.

And the team?

No longer blind.

They had learned to **see what machines whisper in waves.**

More Surprises

While the hardware team was firefighting I^2C errors, Akshay noticed something odd in the logs.

"Guys, we have a memory leak in the parser. Look at the heap, it is growing every time we receive data."

"That's my code," he sighed. I did not free the buffer after decoding. Rookie mistake.

"That's fine," I assured him. "Finding that now is preferable to during the demonstration."

On the other end, Manasa was working on the data visualisation. She had already mocked up charts for temperature, humidity, and motion.

Send me sample packets, she called out. Let us test this with real-time updates.

Ashwin smirked. "Welcome to sensor hell."

The Day the Boss Did Not Smile

That morning, the office buzzed like a coiled spring, tight, tense, full of energy waiting to be unleashed. Deadlines loomed like distant thunder, and yes, some modules still were not integrated. I had reasons, plenty of them, but I knew excuses do not build trust.

What mattered was not the storm ahead but it was how we faced it. So, I straightened my shoulders, took a deep breath, and walked toward that meeting room with one thought: We will figure this out. We always do.

The boss was present, arms crossed, eyes sharp.

He did not wait long.

"Sateesh, what's going on? This phase should have finished two days ago. I trusted you and your team. Is this how we are going to deliver the project?"

His tone was not just disappointment; it was frustration layered with expectation.

I opened my mouth, trying to explain how we faced unexpected issues with board stability, delays in sensor deliveries, and some code regressions we did not foresee. I knew he was not searching for reasons. He wanted accountability. Progress. Urgency.

"I don't want excuses," he snapped. You are leading this. If things are not going right, it is up to you to fix them. The client will not care what went wrong. They will only care if it is late. So, fix it.

For a moment, I felt the weight of it all pressing down on me. I could see my team just outside the glass door, heads down, still working hard. They trusted me. I could not let this instant break me.

I stood straighter.

"Understood, sir. I take full responsibility. Give me some time. I will sit with the team, re-prioritise, and push through. We'll get it back on track."

He gave me a look that said: This is your shot. Do not waste it.

Back at our workstations, I gathered the team. Their faces said everything they had overheard enough.

"We're behind," I told them honestly. But we are not out. We are going to divide, conquer, and close the gaps. We are capable of this. Let us make this right together.

That evening, as screens glowed late into the night, there was no panic, just purpose. We were a team working hard and making progress.

And I promised myself: next time, I would walk into that room with results, not reasons.

After the boss's scolding, something shifted in the room. Perhaps it stemmed from arrogance, perhaps from stress, but the squad experienced it as well. Blame had no allotted time. Acting is the only option now.

That evening, I called for a quick huddle.

We circled around a whiteboard, still stained with scribbles from our last sprint planning. I cleaned with one swipe and drew three columns: Critical, Blockers, Quick Wins.

"Alright, team," I said, marker in hand, "This is where we are. Now let us decide where we need to be in the next few days."

Lessons in Chaos

For the next few days, we were knee-deep in logs, scopes, bug trackers, and patch files. Frustration? Yes. Fatigue? Absolutely.

But also, growth.

Every bug we fix now is one less nightmare later, I told the team during a late-night coffee break.

And one by one, we squashed them.

The sensors started to behave. Stability was achieved by the graphs. The log remained clear.

One by one, the sensors lit up on the screen. A cheer erupted in the room.

"It's working!" someone shouted.

Smiles, high-fives. A mix of disbelief and joy.

"We've officially entered the integration phase," I said. "From here, it only gets more real."

We were learning not just how to build but how to **debug**, how to **dig deeper**, and how to **stay calm when nothing works**.

Chapter Summary

Chapter 5: Power, Precision & Preparedness

Before you flash your first image or power up your board, there is one thing every true embedded engineer must learn:

How to test, measure, and verify.

In **Chapter 5** of my **Technical Notes**, we shift from code to hardware with the tools that help us see what is really happening under the hood.

Here is what you will learn:

- **What are a Multimeter, CRO, Logic Analyser, and Protocol Decoder?**
  Understand the core tools every embedded developer must master.
- **How to Use Them Effectively**
  Measure voltages, trace signals, decode protocols and catch issues before they become problems.
- **First-Time Board Testing**
  What to check *before* hitting the power switch. From verifying power rails, clock signals and checking pin mappings, learn how to prevent disaster before it starts.

Complete **Chapter 5.** Practice the checks. Know your tools.

Because great debugging does not start with trial and error, it starts with preparation.

This is the phase where developers become engineers.

CHAPTER 6

DEEP DIVE INTO THE BOOT PROCESS

The Battle for the Board

Our bring-up was in full swing, the fresh board humming quietly under test.

"Alright," I mentioned, gently placing the freshly flashed board onto the workbench. Everything looks wonderful. Who is next for testing?

Nikita and Akshay spoke up at once, before I completed what I was saying.

"I need it first," said Nikita, reaching for the USB cable.

"No way," countered Akshay, already half-standing from his chair. "I've been waiting since lunch!"

I raised an eyebrow. "Wow. Did we just trigger a lab-level showdown?"

Nikita crossed her arms. "I must test my SPI interface today. You know how long it takes to get the timing right."

Akshay smirked. "And I must debug the UART output that is crashing the complete system. Priorities."

The team chuckled, watching the back-and-forth escalate like a sitcom scene.

I stepped in, somewhat amused, somewhat referee. "Okay, okay, let us not fry the board or each other. Nikita, you get 30 minutes. Akshay, you are upright after all. But next time, we are writing a scheduler for lab access."

They both smiled; the stress dissolved without delay.

The Calm Before the Boot

It was a sunny Thursday sunrise, with the most recent main boards at last delivered.

The team had trained their eyes on signals and scopes. They had listened to the beeps of continuity and noted bits dancing across logic analysers.

But now… the moment had arrived.

The board sat on the anti-static mat, freshly assembled, untested, and brimming with potential.

"Okay," I said, gathering them around. "We are not powering on yet. First… we *verify*."

Ashwin leaned in. "Checklist?"

I handed over the sheet. "Let us undergo the process. Step by step."

✓ **Power rails verified.**
Manasa called out the readings from the multimeter: "3.3V clean. No spikes."

✓ **No shorts across VCC and GND.**
Nikita checked the board edges again, inspecting solder joints with a jeweller's eye.

✓ **All components seated. No reversed capacitors. No missing pull-ups.**
"Reset line pulled high?" Akshay asked, scanning the datasheet and nodding to himself.

We double-checked everything: oscillator orientation, power sequencing, and boot jumper settings. Then I held up the CRO one last time.

Observe the power rail as we switch on the device. Any sound, any drop, we eliminate that immediately.

The air seemed heavy in there. That was not dread, that was admiration. Respect for the silicon, for the process, for the countless things that could go wrong in a millisecond.

"All clear," I said. "Manasa, give it power."

She reached over, fingers hovering above the switch. We all held our breath.

Click.

The CRO showed a clean power-up curve.

The lab's air felt heavy not with silence, but with anticipation.

I sat rooted to my chair, the terminal glowing dimly in front of me. The board refused to boot properly, throwing a kernel panic every time. Logs scrolled too fast. It has been my third hour in the Device Tree Source, outlining each interrupt, each memory node.

Behind me, the team had gone quiet. Akshay leaned toward Ashwin.

"Still stuck on the DTS?"

"Looks like it," he replied. "But I think he's going deeper this time."

They are right.

I am not simply fixing the DTS now, I am diving into the U-Boot config too. Environment variables did not properly point to the correct kernel image. One wrong bootargs, and the whole setup collapsed.

I fixed the memory map, enabled early printk, adjusted the baud rate, and rebuilt U-Boot.

Reboot. Flash. Monitor.

Still no luck.

I realised the few drivers were not loading. I brought up the kernel config and observed that the setup was correct, but still, the peripheral was not even getting probed. Traced it back to a missing compatible string in the DTS.

I edited again, recompiled the driver as a built-in. This had to be it.

Final flash.

We plugged it in.

A few seconds elapsed as if by magic, and the serial console sprang to life.

U-Boot ...

Ashwin gasped in delight. "It's booting!"

The entire team cheered softly. It is not only a board that powered up, it is his confidence, too.

The board came to life. Boot logs passed gracefully. Kernel up. Drivers initialised.

Ashwin broke the silence:

"He got it. The panic's gone."

I looked up eyes, tired but focused. "Fixing boards isn't magic," I said, almost to myself. "It is war. Between us… and every layer of the system."

And today, we won that battle.

Ashwin stood by his station, holding the board carefully like it was a fragile artefact.

"This is my first board bring-up," he said a bit nervously.

I smiled. "Don't worry, you'll learn faster."

Decoding the Boot: From DTS to Initramfs

The afternoon sun filtered through the blinds, casting long shadows across our lab benches. The air smelled faintly of solder and curiosity.

We had completed another lengthy debugging session. The board is finally booting; however, a couple of strange things still lingered, an LED that blinked only after mounting. A mysterious file system labelled initramfs, and a folder named boot that held far more secrets than it appeared.

Akshay spun in his chair and looked over. "Sateesh… what is this .dts file? I keep seeing it in our build process."

Ashwin joined in, holding a printout of the boot logs. "Yeah, and what is this initramfs the message mentions?" Why do we even need that?

At that moment, Nikita entered, gesturing toward the whiteboard. "Also, why is that LED only blinking after the file system mounts? Gives a haunted sort of vibe.

I could not help but smile.

I leaned forward, picked up a marker, and stood at the whiteboard.

Alright. Let us start with a tale regarding how the kernel is aware of the hardware it is communicating with.

Their eyes lit up.

"The DTS, or Device Tree Source, is like a treasure map for the kernel. That informs the kernel of all locations, memory, devices, GPIOs, and clocks. Absent of that, the kernel is blind.

"And the initramfs?" Akshay asked.

"Consider this a short-term root filesystem," I said. This gets used in the initial boot before the actual root filesystem gets mounted. It is like giving the kernel a backpack full of tools to survive the journey until it finds a home.

Ashwin raised an eyebrow. "So… the LED?"

Controlled by a GPIO driver that only gets initialised after the file system mounts. That is when the system loads user-space scripts, and boom, the LED starts blinking. It is like the system stating, I am alive and ready.

Silence fell… then everyone said, "Ooooh."

I grinned. "Any more haunted devices you want me to explain?"

Laughter filled the room, but I could observe the gears turning, the sparks flying. At this moment, they are not simply listening. They learned.

And hungry for more.

By the end of the day, everyone had taken a turn. Akshay lent a hand with the GPIOs. Manasa explored bootloader configs. Nikita shared tips from her past projects.

Everyone, once mentored, is now mentoring.

It is more than simply a project group.

This made up a backing system. A crew of builders, learners, and believers.

One Debugger, Many Dreams

It was a busy Friday morning in the lab. Energy levels were high, coffee cups half full, and everyone was scrambling to meet their module deadlines before the weekend rolled in. Our single trusty debugger, affectionately named "Flash Gordon", was lying on the table like a prized artefact.

At that moment, Ashwin came in holding his board. "I need the debugger. Now. My code's ready, and I want to see it run."

At the same time, Manasa emerged from the other end of the lab, holding her board like a shield. "Excuse me? I have been waiting since morning. My Android application is nearly ready. I only need to examine it!

They locked eyes.

"Oh no," I muttered, spinning my chair slightly toward the team. "We've got another board brawl."

Ashwin placed his board down with a gentle thunk. I require only 10 minutes. Quick flash and verify.

Manasa narrowed her eyes playfully. "Last time your '10 minutes' turned into a kernel panic and an hour-long fix."

Ashwin smirked. "Blame the DTS, not the developer."

The team burst into laughter. Someone whispered, "Time to build two debuggers…"

I stepped in before it escalated to a GPIO war.

"Alright, peace treaty time," I said, raising both hands. "Manasa, since you were waiting, you get first go, but only 20 minutes. Ashwin, you are up right after. And if anyone blows up Flash Gordon, they owe the team pizza."

They both laughed;the tension diffused.

"Deal," said Manasa.

"Fine, but I get to pick the toppings," Ashwin added with a wink.

As the debugger clicked into place and the flashing began, I leaned back in my chair, smiling. Competition or not, this was the spark of a team pushing each other forward, friendships, and all.

Chapter Summary

Chapter 6: Deep Dive into the Boot Process – Get Ready!

Before we move to the next milestone, make sure you have mastered these essentials from my **Technical Notes**:

- **Why does the DTS (Device Tree Source) matter?**
  Understand how the DTS file defines hardware components and communicates with the kernel. It is the blueprint that tells Linux what your board looks like.
- **Importance of initramfs**
  Learn why an initial RAM filesystem is critical for booting, loading essential drivers, and preparing your root filesystem for the system to come alive.
- **Role of init scripts**
  Grasp how early user-space scripts control system initialisation, service startup, and the transition to your application environment.

Action Step:

Review these concepts thoroughly in **Chapter 6** of my Technical Notes. They are the foundation for understanding how your board boots from power-on to a working shell, knowledge that separates good developers from great embedded engineers.

CHAPTER 7

WHEN CODE STARTS TALKING

Connecting the Dots: Manasa's First Communication with the Board

The board got booted. The kernel remained stable.

Right now, it is Manasa's opportunity to shine.

She had been quietly building the Android app for weeks, testing layouts, debugging crashes, and wrestling with permissions. But now, her challenge involved talking to the board.

The Wall of Silence

"It's not responding," she said, eyes fixed on the Android debug logs.

"I have sent the packet. But nothing is coming back."

Ashwin looked over her shoulder. "Did you try pinging it from the board?"

"Yeah. No luck."

I pulled up a chair. Let us start simple. Can you show me your packet format?

She opened the code. Neatly written, structured, but something was off.

"Looks like you're sending it to port 5000," I said. "But on Linux, our listener is on 8080. Let us fix that."

Click. Save. Rebuild.

"Now check the firewall," I added. Linux sometimes blocks incoming connections unless configured.

A few iptables rules later, the board blinked. Literally.

The tiny LED next to the Ethernet port flashed, and Manasa gasped.

The First Handshake

"I got a response!"

The console showed:

{"status: "connected","board_id": "A12X3"}

She leaned back and grinned. "It's working."

The whole team clapped. Even Akshay, usually buried in kernel configs, gave her a high five.

That night, we celebrated more than just a working connection.

We celebrated the **joining of two worlds:** hardware and software, board and app, code and courage.

The 230V Lesson

It happened on a rainy afternoon in the lab. The boards scattered across the desk were some half-soldered, some ready for testing, and one neatly laid out on the anti-static mat: **Nikita's board**. She had spent weeks debugging that board, carefully tracing signals and re-checking every pinout until it finally worked reliably.

That is when Akshay, always eager to move fast, grabbed the adapter without thinking twice. He was supposed to connect to the regulated 5V supply. But in the tangle of cables and sockets, one wrong plug betrayed him. That is the **230V** mains.

A faint click, a sudden *spark*, and then silence. The smell of burnt epoxy filled the air before anyone had time to react. The room froze. Nikita's eyes widened, horror mixing with disbelief. Her board, the one she had nursed through endless nights of testing, was gone in an instant.

"Yaar… I thought it was the adapter!" Akshay stammered, his hands still trembling.

No one shouted. Silence existed, heavier than anger. Nikita sat down, staring at the charred corner of her board. The copper traces were blackened; components fused like melted wax.

I knew this signified a turning point for the team. Mistakes in embedded systems cost more than the time they take, losing the work you have invested yourself in. However, I noticed on Akshay's face that it was not recklessness. It represented a lesson in caution, the kind you never forget.

So instead of blame, I reminded everyone of one thing: *"Every engineer has that one mistake* they will *never repeat. Today, Akshay has earned his."*

Nikita, still upset, managed a faint smile. "Fine. But next time, I get to label all the power supplies."

The team laughed, tension broken. With that, a scorched circuit board evolved into a shared memory, a sign that in engineering, you do not simply construct circuits. You build resilience.

The Report That Spoke Volumes

The moment arrived.

After sleepless weeks and relentless debugging. The team squashed bugs, unblocked ports, and traced logic line by line.

The LED flashes, console logs were clear, and the board turned out alive and stable. It received communication from the app, and the sensor's response seemed clear.

At present, all that remained… existed to face the boss.

The Walk to the Meeting Room

As I walked toward the meeting room, my bag felt heavier than usual. Contained within: logs, screenshots, schematics, plus the debugging report we had painstakingly compiled. Each page told a story not just of technical fixes, but of teamwork, frustration, breakthroughs, and perseverance.

I glanced at my teammates Nikita composed and assured, Akshay and Ashwin with their hands still a little smeared from the previous night's board testing, Manasa clutching her laptop like it had been her sword.

We entered.

The Presentation

The boss looked up. "So, how are things progressing?"

I smiled. "We'd like to show you."

Slide by slide, we took him through:

- **The initial boot failures** — logs that ended in kernel panic.
- **The bug hunt** — wrong GPIO mappings, mismatched voltages, overlooked dependencies.
- **The breakthrough** — a clean boot sequence.
- **The app handshake** — Manasa's proud moment.
- **Sensor response verification** — Akshay showed oscilloscope screenshots like they were trophies.
- **Lessons learned** — debug techniques, hardware discipline, and how a multimeter saved a day.

He listened carefully, asked a few sharp questions and nodded.

"Well done," he said finally. You did not just make it function; you comprehended it. That matters.

The room was silent for a beat.

He continued, Prepare for phase two. I think we can trust this team with more.

As we walked out, we did not cheer. We did not need to.

The serene self-assurance spoke volumes.

We had arrived.

This is Not Our Problem: Clash Between Teams

The bug showed up late in the cycle. The software ran well on the dev kits, but on the custom hardware boards, something seemed off. Random resets, strange I/O behaviour, and peripherals freezing without warning.

The hardware team pointed fingers at us.

"Your code is crashing the system," they argued, waving the logs.

Our team shot back just as firmly.

"No, this is not our problem. The logs show the voltage dipping. That is a hardware fault, not software."

The lab turned into a battlefield. Oscilloscopes got dragged out, traces captured, test cases repeated. Each side defended their ground. For the hardware engineers, acknowledging a design flaw equalled defeat. To us, admitting a software bug appeared as a failure.

The truth, as always, existed somewhere in between. The reset circuit improperly handled brown-out states, and our firmware lacked robustness for a graceful recovery. Hardware and software had collided, and the system suffered for it.

I remember stepping in, looking around at the tired faces of both teams.

"We can keep fighting, or we can fix this." It is not important to the board whose fault it is. Neither will the customer.

Though the silence that followed felt heavy, it broke the tension. Slowly, both teams leaned in together, grudgingly at first, then with full focus. Schematics got rechecked. Firmware got a patch. The system became stable by morning.

The lesson was clear: **in embedded systems, 'not my problem' is the fastest way to kill a project.**

Talking in Silence: How Processes Exchange Information

It was a regular Wednesday, and the energy in the lab was high. The team was deep into developing the software for our embedded device, sensor modules were ready, display logic was shaping up, and data logging was half-built.

But then… things stopped making sense.

Ashwin frowned at his screen. "The sensor values aren't showing up on the display."

Akshay chimed in, "Data's being logged, but the interface has no clue what's going on."

I walked over, took one look at the screen, and smiled knowingly. "Looks like our processes forgot how to talk to each other."

Manasa raised her brow. "Processes… talk?"

"Exactly," "Imagine each part of your software is a team member. One collects sensor data, another formats it, and another shows it to the user. What happens if no one shares updates?"

"They go blind," Nikita answered, catching on.

"In software, the communication between independent processes is called **inter-process communication or IPC.** Without it, each module lives in isolation. They work… but not together."

I scribbled on the whiteboard: **Pipes, Message Queues, Shared Memory, Sockets, Semaphores.**

These are the languages our processes use. Whether you are streaming temperature data, triggering events, or signalling a status, IPC ensures that your system works as a team, not as strangers.

Akshay leaned in. "So, that's why my logger had data, but the UI was clueless…"

"Yep. That is only the start. Choose the right IPC wisely because speed, memory, and complexity all depend on it."

The room fell quiet, gears turning.

"Alright," I said, tapping the board, "Let's make our code start talking."

- **Pipes/FIFOs**
- **Message Queues**
- **Shared Memory**
- **Semaphores**
- **Sockets**

Each came with its own power and pitfalls.

Akshay Dives into Pipes

Akshay was the first to try. He created a pair of small programs, one that sent data, another that read from a pipe.

"It's working!" he smiled. "But it's one-way…"

"Try a FIFO next," I suggested. "Afterward, we can decouple them."

Ashwin Experiments with Message Queues

Ashwin found a way to queue structured messages with priorities.

"It's like sending tiny packets between groups," he joked.

Nikita and Shared Memory

Nikita did not find the latency satisfactory.

"Why are we copying data multiple times?"

"Good point. Let us try shared memory."

She wrote a sample app that used shmget() and shmat() to write sensor data, while another read it.

Bringing It All Together

We combined the pieces into our test application:

- A **sensor module** writing to shared memory
- A **processing module** reads it with semaphores
- A **logging module** receives alerts through message queues
- A **UI updater** using sockets for remote display

Everything worked seamlessly. Every process had its job, and IPC stitched the system into one heartbeat.

As the sun dipped, I looked around the room. The team was not only coding, they orchestrated a symphony of cooperating components.

"Great work, team. Our modules are not isolated anymore, they are talking like us."

Everyone smiled. We had built more than code. We had built a communication system.

When the Processes Stopped Talking

A few days had passed since we stitched together our IPC-driven architecture. Processes were talking, modules were humming, and logs were flowing like clockwork. But something occurred no one enjoys in fixed systems.

Silence.

The logging module stopped receiving updates. The UI froze. A backlog of sensor data piled up like a jammed printer queue.

I gathered the team.

"Looks like one of our IPC channels went down," I said. "Time to make this system robust, not only functional."

Ashwin was deep in the message queue code.

The producer is fine, but what if the queue is full and no one is reading?

"That is the issue," I replied. "We need timeouts and failure recovery."

We updated the msgsnd() and msgrcv() calls with non-blocking modes and retries. Ashwin added fallback logging to prevent silent data loss.

Meanwhile, Nikita proposed an elegant idea.

"Let's add heartbeats between the UI and backend, simple socket pings every few seconds."

"If the heartbeat fails," she added, "we assume the client's gone and re-initialise the connection."

It worked beautifully. We even visualised heartbeat states in our debug logs.

Manasa suggested:

"Why not show this on a live dashboard? Like CPU load, message queue size, and heartbeat states?"

She spun up a lightweight dashboard using a local web server and rendered shared memory stats, logs from sockets, and message queue traffic in near real-time.

Right now, not only could we sense the system, but we could also view it.

To test everything, we simulated failure cases:

- Killed a process mid-execution
- Overloaded message queues
- Froze a socket client
- Injected corrupted shared memory

Each time, our system either recovered, logged a meaningful error, or restarted the affected module.

That evening, I stood before the team:

Great work. We did not simply build IPC, we built strength. This setup is not only living. It recognises when someone hurts it, and it knows how to heal.

The whiteboard now had red, green, and yellow blocks status indicators, retries, and watchdog triggers. It looked less like an architecture diagram and more like a living nervous system.

Chapter Summary

Chapter 7: When Code Starts Talking

You have written functions. You have controlled the hardware. Now it is time to make processes talk because in the world of embedded systems, communication is everything.

Chapter 7 of my **Technical Notes** dives into one of the most critical concepts:

Inter-process Communication (IPC)

Here is what you will explore and master:

- **What is IPC?**
  Why processes need to communicate, and how to do it safely and efficiently.
- **Pipes & FIFOs**
  Streamlined communication is simple, fast, and powerful.
- **Message Queues**
  Send and receive structured data with reliability and control.

- **Shared Memory**
  The quickest method to share, but only if you synchronise precisely.
- **Sockets**
  Establish communication not only between processes but across systems.

Complete **Chapter 7.** Try the code. Understand the flow.

Since builders not only build real-time systems, but they also coordinate them.

This chapter is not only about composing code, it is about planning collaboration.

"Let the processes talk. And let your confidence grow. "

CHAPTER 8

THE BRILLIANCE OF A SYSTEM LIES IN THE INVISIBLE MAGIC OF ITS BUILD

The Build Begins

Alright, team, new phase, new challenge. We are setting up the entire build environment now. Not just patching or flashing. This is where our firmware will be born from source to image.

Nikita chimed in with her usual precision. "Toolchains, feeds, dependencies, scripts we'll need to make this bulletproof."

Akshay and Ashwin glanced at each other, both eager yet nervous. "Time to leave behind pre-compiled binaries," Ashwin said, half-joking.

I handed out the tasks:

- **Nikita**: Define the folder structure and make the initial build reproducible.
- **Manasa**: Document each command.
- **Akshay and Ashwin**: Take charge of dependency installation and toolchain configuration for multiple host systems. Handle local package feeds and verify builds on fresh machines.

Permission Denied: The Day sudo Broke Our Spirits

It started like any other development morning, terminal windows blooming across every monitor. The team was gearing up to install essential packages for our next sprint.

Akshay typed in the command and hit enter.

sudo apt-get install <package>

Boom.

"User is not in the sudoers file. This incident will be reported."

We all froze.

Nikita tried next. Same error.

Manasa gave it a shot, with an annoyed expression. Again denied.

"Wait, are we... locked out of installing packages?" She said, blinking in disbelief.

"Yes," Ashwin confirmed after a quick check. "The admin team revoked elevated privileges last night. Admin team sandboxed us.

The room fell into confused silence.

"We can't even update any packages…" Akshay muttered.

Nikita flopped into her chair. "This is like asking us to race a car but not letting us fill gas."

Grumbling ensued. Someone half-joked, "Next, they'll block CD and tell us to code in Notepad."

I stepped in, trying to lift the mood. "Okay, okay. We have hit a wall. But complaining will not fix it. Let me speak to IT and explain that this is not just about access, it is about ability."

Later that afternoon, I sat with the admin lead and showed them our stack, our needs, and our timelines. I explained the risks of not having proper tools and how we could maintain responsibility without compromising security.

The next day, the mail arrived:

"Selective sudo access granted to embedded team under controlled policy."

The cheers in our lab.

We did not just get privileges, we earned trust.

Trial by Compilation

Subsequently, there came lengthy durations of terminal logs flashing, unending error traces, libraries not present, and version disagreements.

Bit by bit, we began shaping it.
A build system that worked.
The system was rebuilt using a command.
That pulled the correct feed.
That left no mess.

We set up **build profiles**, integrated **custom packages**, and finally… compiled a clean, bootable image from scratch.

When we ran make -j$(nproc) and saw the final image flash green on the board. It felt like viewing a star coming into existence.

I looked around at my team.

Nobody inquired about the next steps.
All stayed occupied in executing.

We became more than contributors. We acted as builders and architects of the system.

And Phase Two? It had recently started.

Where Do We Sit Now?

It existed past 1:00 PM, the time when hunger peaked and the office cafeteria turned into a battlefield.

As usual, our team made a beeline for the cafeteria, trays in hand and laughter trailing behind. However, a change occurred today.

"Why is it so packed?" Ashwin asked, scanning the rows of occupied tables.

Abhishek squinted. "Are they hosting a mini conference here?"

Jayalaxmi stood frozen with her plate. "That's our usual spot… gone."

We walked around twice. Every corner got claimed by people from other departments, interns in clusters, even a few folks holding tables hostage with just coffee mugs and laptops.

"This is ridiculous," Nikita muttered. "We write kernel modules, but we can't even find a table to eat at."

I chuckled and said, "Alright, guerrilla mode. Half of us grab chairs. The rest, grab that free window ledge. Akshay, guard that coffee table like it is the last UART port!"

Somehow, we pieced together a weird little island of stools, corners, and a single shared bench. It felt uneasy, but we existed jointly, joking between bites, consuming off mismatched surfaces like rebels with a code.

Sharpening the Tools: Making the Build System Smarter

The build system was functional, but functional was not enough anymore.

One morning, as we gathered around the whiteboard with mugs of coffee and lingering yawns, I broke the silence.

Team, we have done well. But now it is time to level up. We need a smarter build system. One that understands our needs. One that can help us debug faster, build cleaner, and switch between debug and release without tearing our hair out.

Ashwin raised an eyebrow, half-smiling. "You mean… no more manually editing flags in random Makefiles?"

"You are correct."

The Push for Better

We sat down and listed everything our system lacked:

- Proper **debug vs. release** build separation
- **Compiler flags** that could surface hidden bugs
- A way to **trace issues** deeper into the code
- **Makefile optimisations** that would not break under pressure

- And for packages using **CMake,** a structured configuration system

Nikita, ever the strategist, suggested, "Let's add -Wall -Wextra -Werror -g3 -O0 for debug, and -O2 -DNDEBUG for release builds."

Akshay chimed in, "And wrap it in a script with environment detection, so no one has to remember it all."

We split the tasks:

- **Manasa** started documenting standard build targets.
- **Ashwin and Akshay** worked on template Makefiles and CMake toolchain files.
- **Nikita and I** integrated logging enhancements to track issues from boot to services and focused on adding make targets like:
    - make debug
    - make release
    - make clean && make VERBOSE=1

Chapter Summary

Chapter 8: The brilliance of a system lies in the invisible magic of its build

You have written the code. You have planned the architecture. Now it is time to bring it all together **to build it.**

In **Chapter 8** of my **Technical Notes**, we shift focus to the unsung hero of every software project: the **Build System**. This is where raw code becomes real output,where structure, optimisation, and automation come alive.

Here is what you will uncover:

- **What is a Build System in a Project?**

Understand how to organise and manage source files, dependencies, and targets.

- **Compiler Flags**
  Learn how to control optimisation, debugging, warnings, architecture targeting, and more with precision.

- **Makefile**
  Your first real tool for automating builds. Grasp the syntax, dependencies, variables, and targets that keep your project clean and maintainable.

- **CMake**
  A more scalable, cross-platform way to generate makefiles and manage complex builds. Essential when your project starts growing.

Complete **Chapter 8.** Do not just read, build something**.**

Because engineers do not just code, they craft reliable, repeatable systems that scale.

"Build smart. Build fast. Build right."

CHAPTER 9

BEYOND THE FLASH - UNDERSTANDING WHAT YOU BUILD

Teacher of the Interns: With a Target on My Back

It began simply as another Thursday. I clarified the SPI bus logic to an intern, obviously new but willing to learn. I walked her through MOSI, MISO, clock polarity, the usual stuff.

Behind me, I sensed it.

That smile.

That whisper.

That… chuckle.

I pivoted to view Akshay resting against the lab bench, arms crossed dramatically. "Sateesh sir," he said with mock seriousness, "you have become very dedicated to the intern training program. Especially… certain interns."

Nikita chimed in, "Do you offer weekend coaching too? Asking for a friend."

Manasa smirked, "No wonder the oscilloscope never returns to the shelf, it's always busy during exclusive training sessions."

Jayalaxmi added, "We should rename the board: **Devboard-LoveYou** edition."

I laughed, raising my hands. "She asked for help with SPI. What should I do ,escape?

Akshay grinned. "SPI, you say? Looks more like 'Sateesh's Personal Intern'."

The room erupted.

I shook my head, smiling. "Fine, I will make it official. I invite everyone to the next session. We will call it 'Sateesh's School for Embedded Enthusiasts'."

Ashwin clapped. "With a waiting list, I'm sure."

We were all laughing, and deep down, I felt fortunate that the team had great closeness. Teasing composed a piece of our connection.

For the next few days, the lab buzzed with focused energy.

The build directory now had a structure: debug, release, logs, and toolchains.

When Akshay hit "build" and saw two clean folders populate. Each with the right flags and logs. He let out a relieved sigh.

I looked at the board. Just as our firmware had not evolved alone, our mindset had too.

We are not only composing instructions any longer. We were shaping the tools that shaped our code.

That is how one makes reliable systems not only through commands, but with care.

Unpacking the Binary: The Secrets Hidden in Our Executables

It was a Friday afternoon. The kind where work slows down and curiosity takes over.

After stabilising our build system, the build had completed. Before flashing our latest image onto a test board.

I needed the team to learn not simply what we built but also what we were creating.

"Okay, team," I stated, concluding my laptop with emphasis.

We had been heads-down for weeks, firmware, drivers, board bring-up, test scripts… it was time to zoom out.

I stood in front of the whiteboard, marker in hand.

"We have been building firmware, sure. But how much do you actually know about the binaries we are flashing?

There was a pause.

Akshay raised his hand halfway.

"Yeah, they run. And sometimes… they run *away* with my weekend."

I laughed. "Honestly, what do you think happens when you flash that .bin file?"

Nikita jumped in, crossing her arms. "They boot, run and then do whatever they want?"

"Exactly," Akshay nodded seriously. "Like teenagers."

Everyone laughed.

Okay, okay. We are going to decode that mystery today. From ELF headers to memory mapping. Since we do not create software only for flashing LEDs nowadays.

But let us go deeper.

Opening the Black Box

I held up one of our output files, my_app.

This binary holds everything our logic, our libraries, our functions. But it is not magic. It is just structured data.

We began with the file:

file my_app

Ashwin read it aloud.

"ELF 32-bit LSB executable, ARM, dynamically linked…"

"Notice that?" I spoke. "One command, and now we find that it is an ELF file, created for the ARM architecture. If we accidentally make it for x86, this command informs us swiftly.

Next: size

size my_app

Manasa tilted her head. "Text, data, bss… what's all this?"

I smiled. That is our code. The text segment is your instructions. data segment is your initialised variables. bss is uninitialized. Want to keep memory tight? Start by watching these numbers.

Then: nm

nm my_app | grep ' T '

"Whoa," Abhishek said, eyes widening as a long list of function names scrolled by.

"Yep," I said. nm shows all the symbols in your binary. Want to find out if your function got compiled in? This is your go-to. Also, handy when linking fails.

Finally: strings

strings my_app | less

Akshay detected something without delay.

"Wait... that's our debug message!"

"Exactly. strings helps you see human-readable content in the binary. Forgot to remove that embarrassing log line? This will show it."

The Bigger Picture

By the end of the session, our simple binary had become an open design filled with awareness instead of a mystery.

At that moment, I detected a change in the squad's expressions beyond curiosity, but control.

They were not just developers any longer.

They were becoming embedded engineers.

Now the room was buzzing with anticipation.

The team had checked the connections twice, verified the build, and reviewed the boot log from the previous attempt. Everything looked good on paper.

"Alright," I said, looking at Akshay. "You are up. Let us flash our newly built image."

He cracked his knuckles theatrically, grinning. "Here goes nothing."

With a few keystrokes, the image began transferring. Everyone leaned in, watching the terminal as if it were a suspense thriller.

Transfer complete.

The prompt returned. No errors. Only quiet.

"Done," Akshay said. "That's in."

We waited.

One second. Two. Five.

Ashwin looked over. "Why it is not booting?"

I moved closer to the board. No LEDs. No serial output. Only... silence.

Akshay frowned. "But… the image flashed successfully."

Abhishek mentioned, "Maybe it is simply shy."

Nikita raised an eyebrow. "Did we… break it?"

I sighed, already reaching for the serial cable. "Alright, let us go deeper. U-Boot logs, DTS config, kernel parameters somewhere, something is off."

The team huddled closer. The real debugging had only begun.

I connected the serial cable and opened the terminal. The screen stayed dark for some seconds… finally, U-Boot logs began to scroll.

"Okay," I muttered, squinting at the bootloader output. "At least we know U-Boot's alive."

Ashwin leaned over. "But why didn't the kernel load?"

I paused the log and pointed to a line.

"Right here, see this? It is trying to boot from memory offset 0x84000000, but we flashed our image at 0x81000000. Wrong address."

Akshay scratched his head. "So, the kernel's… simply sitting there? Waiting for someone to knock?"

"Exactly," That is like guiding someone to an incorrect location and questioning why they do not reach the destination.

We reconfigured U-Boot to match the correct load address, and just as I hit save, Nikita noticed something else.

"Wait, what's this warning about the DTB not being found?"

I nodded. "Good catch. That is the Device Tree blob, the blob tells the kernel about the hardware layout. No DTB, no idea where the hardware is. One is operating without information.

Ashwin jumped in. "Possibly that is why the LED was not blinking after mounting. That was not even aware of LEDs.

The group erupted into laughter; however, the statement stood correct.

We fixed the address, pointed U-Boot to the correct DTB, and repackaged the image.

“Alright,” I mentioned, and returned it to Akshay. Try flashing once more. This time, we have all the pieces in place.

He nodded, more serious this time.

The image flashed.

The board booted.

A heartbeat LED blinked on.

A serial log greeted us: Boot successful.

The room erupted in cheers.

Ashwin clapped. “We revived a dead board.”

“Not dead,” I said, smiling. Only misinterpreted.

Chapter Summary

Chapter 9: Beyond the Flash – Understanding What You Build

We have been building firmware, sure. But how much do you truly understand regarding the binaries we are flashing?

It was you who wrote the code. You did the assembly. You flashed binary.

Hold on and ponder what really went into such a binary.

What mysteries does it hide? What size, symbols, and strings make it tick?

My **Technical Notes** in **Chapter 9** reveal hidden aspects of your firmware, aspects able to build or destroy a system.

Here is what you will learn:

- **What Really Happens When You Flash That** .bin **File?**

Understand memory mapping, layout, headers, and how bootloaders interpret what you flash.

- **Using** file, size, nm, **and** strings **commands**

Peek inside the binary.

file – Know what kind of executable you are dealing with

size – see how much space your code really takes

nm – Explore symbols, functions, and addresses

strings – Discover what data lives inside

Complete **Chapter 9. Make it a habit to inspect what you build.**

Because true embedded engineers do not just write code, they **understand** what runs on the hardware. That is not only flashing firmware that is flashing confidence.

CHAPTER 10

DECODE THE INVISIBLE - TOOLS THAT UNCOVER THE TRUTH

Beyond the Crash: GDB and readelf for Real Debugging

The board had booted, but something was off.

Our personalised application crashed upon starting. No logs. No clues. Just silence.

"Alright," I said, gathering the team. "This is where the fun begins."

Ashwin leaned forward. "What's the plan?"

I walked to the whiteboard and wrote two words: readelf, gdb.

"These two," I began, "are about to be your best friends."

Nikita frowned. "But the code compiles. Isn't that enough?"

"If that compiled right," I stated, opening my terminal, "why did that fail when starting?"

I ran readelf -h my_app.elf.

"First," I pointed out, "this tells us everything about the binary architecture, entry point, segments, and more. Hey, look at this. Our binary is built for the wrong architecture variant. That is strike one."

Akshay's eyes widened. "So, we're feeding the processor an accent that it doesn't understand?"

"Definitely."

We fixed it, and next, I loaded the binary into GDB with the core file from the crash.

"Let us step through and determine where the program fails," I stated, hitting start.

Line by line, the debugger walked through the code, until… boom. Segmentation fault on a null pointer.

"That's it," I expressed, highlighting the line. "Uninitialized structure. We assumed the pointer was valid."

Ashwin nodded slowly. "And we'd never have found this without GDB?"

"Not without guessing for hours."

By the end of the session, the team was silent but in awe.

"This," I said, pointing at the debugger window, "is where code stops being a black box. You do not just run programs anymore. You dissect them."

Akshay laughed. "It's like we've unlocked a new superpower."

Nikita smirked. "Forget logs. GDB is therapy for misbehaving binaries."

We fixed the pointer bug, recompiled with the correct flags, and flashed the image again.

This time, the app ran. Smooth. Stable. Clean.

Ashwin clapped. "Debugger saves the day."

The board was up. The binary was running. But something still was not right.

Why does it take so long? Nikita inquired, spotting the device's lag during input handling.

Ashwin nodded. "And it is eating processor like crazy."

I pulled my chair closer. "Alright, time to go deeper. Today, we will meet another powerful command: **strace**.

Akshay raised an eyebrow. "More debugging tools?"

"No," I grinned. "This does not debug your code. That reveals what your code does to the system.

I fired up strace and ran our binary.

"Note this," I mentioned. "strace displays each syscall—open, read, write, mmap, ioctl… everything."

As the screen scrolled, the team leaned in.

"Check out these standard open calls?" I pointed. We are opening the same config file 30 times a minute. That is inefficient.

"Wow," Nikita murmured. "No wonder there's an inflated feeling."

Akshay was stunned. "That's like… X-ray vision for the system."

I nodded. Correct. strace shows you what your app asks of the kernel.

We fixed the inefficiencies, committed the changes.

Nikita stretched. "It's like we're finally talking to the system and it's answering back."

Chapter Summary

Chapter 10: Decode the Invisible – Tools That Uncover the Truth

You have written the code. You have built a binary.

But if things fail, do you understand how to trace the fault line?

Chapter 10 of my **Technical Notes** introduces you to the powerful tools every systems engineer must master to see what is really happening beneath the surface.

Here is what you will learn:

- **GDB (GNU Debugger)**
  Step through your code. Set breakpoints. Inspect variables. Fix the unfixable.
- **readelf**
  Explore ELF headers, section tables, and symbol mappings to gain clarity on how your binary is structured.
- **strace**
  Track every system call your program makes. Need to discover what is going on once your application stops working or goes down? Start here.

Complete **Chapter 10. Do not just memorise ;practice commands with intent.**

Because understanding **how your code behaves at runtime separates** programmers from problem solvers.

In debugging, knowledge is power. These tools are your flashlight in the dark.

CHAPTER 11

FIND THE FLAWS BEFORE THEY FIND YOU

Ghost in the Memory: Enter Valgrind

It started as a slow week subtle, invisible. The board would boot fine, the app would run, but after a few minutes, things would drift.

"Nikita," I asked, looking over her shoulder, "why is the heap usage climbing on every sensor read?"

She shrugged. "I have been freeing everything I malloc'd. I double-checked."

Akshay chimed in, "Maybe the library's buggy?"

"No," I said, pulling my chair in. "It is time we meet a very precise investigator. Team, say hello to *Valgrind*."

"Sounds intense," Ashwin smirked.

"Yes, it is. "Valgrind watches every memory allocation, every deallocation, every leak. Like a detective who never sleeps."

I built the binary with debug symbols and ran:

valgrind --leak-check=full ./sensor_app

The terminal came alive with logs.

"Look here," I pointed. "See this? 'definitely lost: 64 bytes in 2 blocks.' That means something you malloc'd is never freed."

We traced the log. There it was inside the temperature sensor parser, a strdup() without a corresponding free().

Nikita's eyes widened. "I missed that completely."

"That's the thing about memory leaks," I said. "They do not always crash your code. They just wait quietly, eating your system alive."

We cleaned it up, recompiled, and ran Valgrind again.

All heap blocks are now free; no leaks are possible.

Ashwin grinned. "Now that's satisfying."

Akshay leaned back. "Why didn't we learn this earlier?"

"And from here on, Valgrind is your shadow. It will follow your code into every corner."

The team nodded, absorbing not just a new tool but a mindset.

The room was too quiet for a dev lab. Everyone focused, and the ghost of one final bug haunted them. The system ran clean with Valgrind, but memory usage still grew suspiciously high over time.

"Okay," I said, clapping once. "Valgrind's leak-check passed. However, what if the application is consuming considerable memory by design? Not leaking simply... bloating?"

Ashwin frowned. "So, like a memory diet problem?"

"Yes, it is time to bring in *Massif.* It is Valgrind's profiler cousin."

I typed:

valgrind --tool=massif ./sensor_app

ms_print massif.out.<pid>

The output showed a detailed breakdown of each heap allocation tracked over time, with call stacks.

"There," I pointed. Check your sensor buffer huge chunk. But examine closer: the string tokenizer's copy function, it is duplicating every sample.

"Do we need to?" Nikita asked.

Nope. Simply parse in-place.

With a quick refactor, and memory usage dropped by 40%.

"Alright," Akshay said, "we're slimming down."

"But let's not stop at runtime," I said. "We can examine our code before it compiles."

Team with curiosity how it is possible before compilation?

It is a surprise. Let us hold off until the next session.

Seeing the Bugs Before They Bite

The office was buzzing with the usual debugging chaos: boards plugged in, logs scrolling endlessly across terminals, and the occasional sigh from someone who had just hit yet another segmentation fault.

I gathered the team. "Guys, let me ask you this: what if we could catch some of these bugs *before* we even run the code?"

Akshay raised an eyebrow. "You mean… like magic?"

I grinned. "Not magic. Static analysis."

I opened my laptop and pulled up a small C program. "Look here," I said, pointing at a function. "No warnings, it compiles fine. But what if I told you this could cause a memory leak?"

Ashwin frowned. "But the compiler didn't say anything."

"You are right," "Compilers check for syntax and a few basic rules. But they do not care about deeper logic, unused variables, memory leaks, or null pointer dereferences. That is where **static analysis tools** come in."

I typed in:

cppcheck main.c

Errors and warnings filled the screen, things the compiler had happily ignored.

Nikita leaned forward. "So Cppcheck reads the code like… a super-strict reviewer?"

"Perfect analogy," I nodded. "It does not run the program. It *analyses* the code paths, variables, and patterns. It finds mistakes before they even become runtime crashes."

Manasa scribbled in her notebook. "So, if we use this before testing, we save time chasing bugs later?"

"Yes,". "Think of it like a doctor doing preventive checkups instead of waiting until the patient collapses. Static analysis tools like Cppcheck, Coverity, or Clang Static Analyser give us early warnings. They do not replace testing, but they make our lives a lot easier."

The team exchanged looks. The exhaustion on their faces softened into curiosity. For once, debugging did not feel like endless firefighting; it felt like we had a new shield.

During the day, the group included cppcheck within the checklist before commit.

Nikita smiled. "Cold and beautiful."

We cleared warnings one by one, sharpening the codebase like polishing armour before battle.

By the end of the day, we had a clean heap profile, no leaks, and a codebase pre-checked for subtle bugs.

You have seen what runtime tools do. You have seen what static tools do. Together, they make you unstoppable.

Akshay leaned back. Feels like we are finally writing production-grade code.

I nodded, saying, "Yes, you are." Welcome to real embedded development.

Chapter Summary

Chapter 11: Find the Flaws Before They Find You

You have built the code. That compiles. That functions. However, does that function correctly?

Does the program leak memory, leave dangling pointers, or carry silent bugs waiting to strike?

Chapter 11 of my **Technical Notes** is about **writing safe, stable, and production-ready code** by mastering the art of **detection before disaster**.

Here is what you will explore:

- **Valgrind**
  Track memory leaks, invalid accesses, and uninitialized variables.
  Understand heap behaviour and stop subtle bugs before they hit production.

- **Static Analysis with Cppcheck**
  Scan your codebase for logical errors, undefined behaviours, and edge-case vulnerabilities without even running the program.

Complete **Chapter 11**. Run your code through these tools.

It is great to write working code, but writing robust, leak-free, maintainable code is what makes you a professional.

CHAPTER 12

THE POWER OF HAL IS IN MAKING HARDWARE SPEAK YOUR LANGUAGE

Beyond the Code: The HR Conversation

It was 4 p.m. when I got the message.

"Sateesh, can you come to the HR cabin for a quick chat?"

I paused. Not a bug report. Not a build failure. HR?

I walked in, and there she was, our HR manager, smiling.

"Sateesh," she began gently, we have noticed you are deeply involved in your project. We appreciate the effort. But… you have not been part of any cultural events, wellness activities, or even the Friday fun hours. The team needs balance. So do you.

I smiled politely, but my mind flashed through the last few weeks: debugging kernel panics, mentoring juniors, coordinating with hardware vendors, testing under pressure. Every hour counted.

I understand. But the project is in a crucial phase. We are creating something completely new. My team depends on me not only to program but to lead, unblock, and be available when stress increases.

She sighed, "I get that. But we also need you to be part of the larger company culture. Even small involvement differs."

I nodded. "How about this? Once the current milestone is stable, I will host a tech quiz during the next Friday fun hour. Let us turn learning into fun."

Her face brightened. "Deal. And maybe one dance performance too?"

I laughed. "Let's not push it."

We both smiled. That conversation did not just recall balance; it recalled that even engineers need to unplug sometimes.

Bridging the Gap: From HAL to Application

The boards were stable. Drivers were working. But now came the real test, building the bridge between hardware and what users experience.

The **HAL Layer** and the **Application Layer**.

I gathered the team around the whiteboard. "Alright, everyone," I began, "our drivers are the muscles. Now it is time to build the brain and the face."

Ashwin raised his hand. "You mean HAL is like the brain?"

Close. HAL, or Hardware Abstraction Layer, acts like a translator. It talks to the hardware in a consistent, clean way, so the application does not need to know what is going on underneath.

Manasa added, "So it's like APIs for hardware?"

"Exactly," I nodded. "Let's split the work."

Team Breakdown

- **Akshay and Ashwin** would focus on building the **HAL layer,** creating clean, testable interfaces for GPIO, I2C, UART, and SPI.

- **Manasa** would start designing the **application layer**, which could talk to HAL, make decisions, update the UI or send messages.
- **Nikita** volunteered to review the HAL interface designs for maintainability and clarity.

Getting Started

"HAL should never contain hardware logic directly," I explained. "Instead, write clean functions like hal_led_on() or hal_sensor_read() that internally use our drivers."

This way, if we change the board, the application will not even notice. That is the magic of abstraction.

Akshay grinned. "So, the app team doesn't need to worry about I2C registers anymore?"

"Yes, You are right. They just call hal_get_temperature() and get back the value."

By the end of the day, the first prototype was running.

- **HAL Layer**:
  - hal_gpio.c/h, hal_uart.c/h, hal_sensor.c/h
- **Application Layer**:
  - main.c handled business logic, logging, and status updates.

When the LED blinked after reading sensor data and transmitting over the network... the room lit up with more than just the LED.

Feels like you guys are building a real system now, Jayalaxmi said quietly.

I smiled. "We are."

Chapter Summary

Chapter 12: The power of HAL is in making hardware speak your language

Your code works, but will it work on a different board tomorrow?

What if the microcontroller changes? Or the hardware interface evolves?

Chapter 12 of my **Technical Notes** introduces one of the most essential pillars of scalable embedded development:

The Hardware Abstraction Layer (HAL)

Here is what you will understand:

- **Why HAL Matters?**
  Separate your application logic from hardware dependencies, write once, scale many.
- **Build Clean Architecture**
  HAL enables portability, testability, and smoother collaboration between software and hardware teams.
- **Simplify Migration & Maintenance**
  Swap out peripherals or platforms with minimal rewrites. Stay agile as hardware evolves.

Complete **Chapter 12.** Grasp the HAL conceptually and in practice.

Engineers design real embedded projects to adapt. Not to survive on only one board.

HAL is not just a layer; it is your foundation for flexibility and futureproofing.

CHAPTER 13

MAKE EVERY CYCLE COUNT - PROFILING & PERFORMANCE TUNING

Racing the Clock: Profiling the Invisible Bottlenecks

The lab was unusually quiet that evening, only the soft hum of our boards and the clatter of keyboards breaking the silence. Everyone was busy with their modules, but I could see the same tension on each face: the code *worked*, but it was not *fast*.

"Alright, team," I said, pulling my chair closer. "It is time to stop guessing where the problem is. Let me show you how we actually measure performance."

Akshay looked up from his screen. "We've been optimising blindly… changing loops, rewriting conditions… but the execution time doesn't improve much."

I nodded. "Exactly. That is like treating a patient without diagnosing them. We need a stethoscope for code performance, and that's where **profiling** comes in."

I opened the terminal and recompiled the program with the -pg flag.

"This tiny flag," I explained, "tells the compiler to insert hooks. Every function call is tracked. When we run the program, the execution flow is recorded."

Nikita leaned forward. "And then what?"

"We feed the data into **gprof**," I said, typing the command. Numbers and percentages filled the screen. "This report tells us which functions consumed the most CPU time. Look, our process_data() takes up nearly 65%. That is our real bottleneck, not the small loops you were worried about."

Ashwin blinked. "So… all this time we were optimising the wrong part of the code?"

"Exactly," I smiled. "Without profiling, you are just poking in the dark. With gprof, you get a map. You stop wasting effort on the 5% functions and focus on the ones that eat 60% of execution time."

Manasa, who had been quiet until now, tapped her notebook. "This means before we optimise, we should always *measure*. Otherwise, we might make the code more complex without real gain."

"That is the golden rule. Never optimise blindly. Always profile first."

The team exchanged nods, the frustration on their faces replaced by curiosity. For the first time that week, I felt the energy in the room shift from tired trial and error to focused, data-driven problem solving.

But how do we see real-time system behaviour? Akshay asked.

"Ah," I smiled. "Time to meet htop, iotop, and even strace."

Each tool gave a different view of CPU utilisation, disk I/O, and system calls in flight.

Performance is not only about rapid code. "It is about *smart* code. Knowing where your CPU is going... and stopping it from going there."

The day ended with a faster, lighter, smarter application.

"You only squeezed seconds out of microseconds," I mentioned proudly. Now imagine doing this across a complete system.

Abhishek grinned. "Feels like we have levelled up."

"You did," I nodded. "Welcome to the art of embedded optimisation."

Chapter Summary

Chapter 13: Make Every Cycle Count – Profiling & Performance Tuning

Your code works. Your system runs.

However, is that sufficiently speedy? Efficient enough? Does the CPU burn, waste cycles, or lag under stress?

Chapter 13 of my **Technical Notes** focuses on optimising your embedded application not just to run, but to **run smart.**

Here is what you will unlock:

- **Importance of CPU Profiling & Performance Tuning**
  Identify bottlenecks. Improve execution time. Optimise power and resource usage.

- **Key Tools You Must Master:**
  - **perf** – Analyse low-level CPU performance metrics.
  - **gprof** – Profile function calls and execution times in your code.
  - **htop** – Visualise CPU usage, process priorities, and load.

- **iotop** – Monitor I/O usage in real time—catch file system slowdowns.

Complete **Chapter 13.** Run the tools. Tune the code.

Because writing code is only half the job. **Running it efficiently is what makes it production-grade.**

Performance is not a bonus; it is a responsibility.

CHAPTER 14

MASTERING CONCURRENCY - THREADS, LOCKS, AND PRIORITIES

The Great Work From Home Debate

It was just after the daily stand-up when I noticed a subtle shift in the team's mood.

The chatter was quieter. People stirred coffee mugs with less enthusiasm. Even Nikita, who habitually cracked a joke by 10 a.m., was strangely quiet.

I subsequently asked, "Okay, what is going on? Everyone looks like someone pushed their code to /dev/null."

Akshay finally spoke up. "It is a WFH thing, Sateesh. Other teams are getting the option. But we have been told no again."

I sighed, leaning back in my chair. "I get it. Trust me, I do. I would love to be debugging device trees from my couch with filter coffee too."

Manasa added, "We are not asking to vanish. Just a couple of days, especially when the hardware's not needed."

They had a point. Some parts of our work needed physical boards, lab tools, and in-person coordination. But not all.

That evening, I forwarded a Word mail to our manager.

The next day, the response came.

"Let's talk. I appreciate the team's dedication. We can work something out."

When I shared the news, the team broke into smiles. Abhishek mock bowed. "Our saviour."

I laughed, "Do not thank me yet. Let us prove remote work does not mean remote responsibility."

And with that, we struck a balance between productivity and peace of mind.

One Core, Too Many Tasks

The system was running leaner now, and CPU cycles trimmed, our memory footprint tighter. But as features stacked up, a new complexity emerged.

The office lights flickered as dusk settled outside. Most of the floor had emptied, but our bay was still alive, keyboards clicking, monitors glowing, coffee cooling.

"Why is the UI lagging again?" Ashwin groaned, slamming his hand on the desk.

"I swear the sensor read loop is blocking it," Akshay replied, spinning around in his chair. "We're polling every 500ms, right in the main thread."

I walked over, sipping what remained of my third coffee. "And what if the UI didn't have to wait for its turn?"

They looked at me, puzzled.

I pulled up a whiteboard.

"Think of it like a restaurant," I began. "Right now, we have one chef doing everything: taking orders, cooking, serving. If one table takes time, the whole restaurant slows down."

Nikita's eyes lit up. "Multithreading?"

"Exactly. We create threads. Assign one for sensor reads, another for UI updates. They work together, not one after the other."

We spent the next hour rewriting the code.

Thread 1 handled sensors.

Thread 2 took care of the display.

Thread 3 logged the data to storage.

And the main thread? It orchestrated them all.

When we ran the program again, the UI flowed like water. No more stuttering. No more freezing. Everything was in harmony.

"That's the magic of Multi-threading," I said, leaning back. Speed is not the only factor. What it is is structure. That expression means "letting parts of your program breathe."

Nikita leaned back and said, "It's like we've mastered time itself."

I laughed. "Welcome to Multithread Programming."

The room seemed brighter not only because the code ran, but because we had passed another landmark in conceiving ideas as truly integrated engineers.

The Code That Froze Without Warning

Two days after we celebrated the smooth multi-threading demo, something went wrong.

It was slightly after 6 a.m. when I got the call.

"Sateesh, the device is not responding again… Same thing as yesterday. It is stuck."

Half-asleep, I rolled out of bed and opened my laptop. The logs stared back at me, frozen. Two threads are waiting on each other like drivers at a four-way stop, neither willing to move first.

A classic **deadlock**.

By 9 a.m., the entire team huddled around the whiteboard. I drew it out:

Thread A → waiting for Resource X

Thread B → holding Resource X, waiting for Resource Y

Thread A → also holding Resource Y.

I looked at Akshay and said, "It's like both of them are holding a key but need the other's key to move."

Ashwin raised his hand. "So… how do we stop this? Prioritise the threads?"

"Not only prioritise," "We **control access**. And that's where **mutexes** and **semaphores** come in."

Manasa blinked. "Like traffic lights?"

"Yes," I smiled. "A **mutex** ensures only one thread is inside a critical section, think of it like a locked door. And a **semaphore** is more like a counting system. It controls how many threads can access a resource at once."

We spent the afternoon refactoring our code.

- Introduced a **mutex** to guard the shared I2C bus.
- Used a **semaphore** to manage sensor read queues.
- Added **timeouts** and **priority handling** for real-time tasks.

By evening, we flashed the firmware. All eyes were on the board.

The LED blinked, sensors responded, data flowed.

No freeze.

Simply harmony.

Ashwin whispered, "It's like we taught the system to breathe again."

I nodded, proud not only of the code, but of the team.

They had not only solved a bug. They had learned the **art of synchronisation**.

In embedded systems, it is not only about writing code that runs, it is about writing code that shares, waits, respects, and never panics.

Chapter Summary

Chapter 14: Mastering Concurrency – Threads, Locks, and Priorities

Time, tasks, and resources are all constrained in embedded systems.

To survive and scale, your code needs to **do more at once without chaos.**

Chapter 14 of my **Technical Notes** will prepare you to harness the full power of **multi-threading and real-time execution.**

Here is what you will explore:

- **Importance of Multithread Programming**
  Break down tasks, improve responsiveness, and build scalable logic with parallel execution.
- **Importance of Mutexes and Semaphores**
  Avoid race conditions. Protect shared data. Synchronise smartly.
- **Importance of Thread Priorities**
  Not all tasks are equal; know which ones must run first, and why. Real-time means right-time.

Complete **Chapter 14. Implement threads, locks, and scheduling with intent.**

Since handling concurrency is not only concerning velocity, it regards command, security, and accuracy.

Compose programs that do not merely execute in parallel; compose programs that execute with intent.

CHAPTER 15

LINKING IT ALL TOGETHER - FILES, LIBRARIES, AND EXECUTION

Threads of Tradition, Ties of Teamwork

The morning sun had not fully crept over the building, but our office floor appeared brighter than usual, and it did not involve just the overhead lights.

It was Ethnic Day.

The usual jeans and hoodies disappeared. In their place stood a kaleidoscope of colours, fabrics, and stories.

Akshay strolled in wearing a crisp kurta, awkwardly adjusting his dupatta like it was a debugging cable.

"Is this supposed to go left, or right?" he asked.

Manasa twirled once in her half-saree, laughing.

"Forget the debugging, let's debug your draping first."

Nikita, in a fusion Indo-western look, walked in with grace and confidence.

"Ethnic. But make it embedded," she winked.

Even Ashwin, Abhishek and Jayalaxmi joined from the other wing, each flaunting their traditional best, the group felt whole again.

We gathered in the lounge for the team photo. No laptops. No whiteboards. Heritage, smiles, and that shared sense of identity. A reminder that behind every developer, there is a story much older than silicon.

But of course, it would not be a team day without some teasing.

"Akshay," someone quipped, "you write better code than you match colours."

"And Sateesh," Nikita added, "next time, maybe try something brighter than beige, yeah?"

I chuckled, sipping chai from an earthen cup. "I'm saving the RGB for Diwali."

There were games, laughter, and even a mini dance-off that no one admitted winning.

But what made the day truly special?

Over a couple of hours, the single thing we put together is, connection. The only thing we flashed were **smiles**.

In the dhol's rhythm and the camera's sound, we became more than engineers originating from different states.

We existed as stories connected, forming a lively, powerful team.

After all the photo, laughter, and tea breaks, someone from HR wheeled in a tiny whiteboard and yelled,

"QUIZ TIME! Culture + Tech = Let us see how ethnic you really are."

The crowd groaned.

Nikita folded her arms. "I swear, if they ask me which state Pongal is from, I'm walking out."

Ashwin whispered to Akshay, "Bet he gets every question wrong but still answers with confidence."

Akshay grinned. “Confidence is half the score.”

Teams got formed. We formed Team Breakpoint. Jayalaxmi, the surprise host, held up the mic.

“Alright! First question. What is the traditional Maharashtrian headwear worn by men called?”

Akshay buzzed in confidently: “Um… Fedora?”

Everyone burst out laughing.

“No, Akshay. That is your *GitHub profile picture*, not a festival hat,” Nikita groaned.

“Okay, okay, next one,” said Jayalaxmi, smirking. “What festival celebrates the victory of god over evil with bonfires and often comes before Holi?”

Manasa hit the buzzer. “Holika Dahan!”

“Correct!” Cheers erupted.

After that came the last question and the surprise.

Jayalaxmi glanced at the card and paused. “Which year marks the first Pongal celebration?”

Silence.

Everyone looked puzzled.

Nikita squinted. “Wait. Even Google does not know that.”

Ashwin teased, “Did you make that up?”

Jayalaxmi blinked, laughed, and said, "Okay, fine! Skip! Even I do not know, I copied it from a meme page."

Laughter exploded. Even the HR manager could not keep a straight face.

Finally, nobody won but the memories.

As we walked back to our desks, I heard someone say.

"That quiz is as precise as our initial effort at composing a device driver."

In a flash, we returned to our roles as engineers.

...somewhat more culturally assured at present.

The Library Dilemma: Static vs Dynamic

It was late afternoon, and the lab was buzzing with quiet concentration. The team was deep into building the application layer when Akshay suddenly frowned at his screen.

"Sateesh, I'm getting linker errors again," he said, turning his monitor towards me. "I think it's because we're not linking the library correctly."

I glanced over. The error logs told me everything I needed to know.

"Alright, team," I said, standing up. It is time for a little detour. Let us gather around. We need to talk about something critical: **libraries**.

The team shifted their chairs closer.

The Concept of Libraries

"Libraries," I began, "are collections of pre-compiled code functions and utilities that we can reuse across projects. They save us from rewriting everything."

There are **two types** we need to understand: **static** and **dynamic**.

Static Libraries

I drew on the whiteboard:

Static Library (.a)

- Gets copied into your final executable at compile time.
- Increases the size of the binary.
- Does not require the library to be present on the system during runtime.

"So, everything is self-contained?" Ashwin asked.

"Exactly," I nodded. "But the downside is that if you update the library, you need to recompile every executable that used it."

Dynamic Libraries

Dynamic Library (.so)

- Linked at runtime, not compile time.
- Keeps the executable size small.
- Makes updating shared code easier, just replace the .so file.

"But there's a catch," I continued. Your system needs to have the right .so files at the right paths; otherwise, your program won't run.

When to Use What

"Use static libraries when you want portability, and don't want to depend on the system having specific files."

"Use dynamic libraries when size matters, or when you want to update shared logic without re-compiling everything."

Nikita was already sketching a plan. So, we can keep our hardware abstraction layer as a static library for now, and maybe make the Message Broker utilities dynamic?

"I smiled. "You're thinking like architects now."

Within a few hours, the errors were gone. The team had built a clean HAL static library and began modularising other components into shared objects.

"Feels lighter and cleaner now," Akshay said.

"Like a library should," I replied.

Links That Bind: Understanding Soft and Hard Links

The project was progressing steadily. Our build system was shaping up, and the team was navigating the embedded environment like pros. That afternoon, while organising files in the build directory, Manasa called out:

"Sateesh, I think I accidentally deleted the source file… but there is still a copy in another folder. How is that possible?"

I smiled. "That is not a copy. That is a **link**. Let me show you something cool."

Gathering the Team

We gathered near the whiteboard, tea mugs in hand.

"In Linux," "a link is like a pointer or shortcut to a file. There are two types: **hard links** and **soft links**."

Nikita leaned in. "What's the difference?"

Hard Links

I wrote:

Hard Link

- Points directly to the **inode** (the data structure that stores file metadata and location).
- Multiple filenames refer to the same content.
- File remains until all hard links are deleted.
- Cannot span across different filesystems.

I demonstrated:

$ ln original.txt hardlink.txt

"Now," "both original.txt and hardlink.txt are the same file. Delete one, the data still exists."

Surprised, Akshay remarked, "So... it's like having multiple doorways to the same room."

Soft (Symbolic) Links

Next, I wrote:

Soft Link (Symbolic Link)

- Points to the filename, **not** the inode.
- Like a shortcut or alias.
- Breaks if the original file is deleted.
- Can span across filesystems.

When to Use What

Use **hard links** when you want file redundancy without extra space.

Use **soft links** when you need flexibility and symbolic references across directories or filesystems.

We went back to the build folder. Manasa's "deleted" file had only been a soft link. We recreated it easily.

"Thanks, Sateesh," she said. "These links are lifesavers."

"Only if you know when to use which," I said with a grin.

Chapter Summary

Chapter 15: Linking It All Together – Files, Libraries, and Execution

You have built binaries, written code, and structured your system, but do you truly understand what connects everything behind the scenes?

Chapter 15 of my **Technical Notes** covers two vital topics that every system and embedded engineer must master:

Linking and Libraries.

Here is what you will learn:

- **Importance of Soft and Hard Links.**
  Understand how the filesystem level references files and how symbolic versus actual inodes influence your project's behaviour and portability.

- **Importance of Static and Dynamic Libraries**
  Understand when to embed code for maximum speed and self-containment (static linking), and when to share for efficiency, flexibility, and modular design (dynamic linking).

Complete **Chapter 15.** Practice creating, linking, and using both.

Because these are not just concepts, they are decisions that impact **performance, memory, and maintainability**.

Behind every efficient system lies the right link.

CHAPTER 16

TRACK IT. SAVE IT. SHARE IT. - THE POWER OF GIT AND DOXYGEN

The First Commit: Planting the Seed

There was a serene afternoon, a kind where the hum of devices and the clicking of keys merged into a beat of committed focus. The team had just wrapped up our initial round of prototyping. The code appeared basic, working, and hopeful. That is not perfect, but it is ours.

I looked around the room.

"Alright, team," "this is our foundation. Let us commit this reference code. That will represent the opening stone for our forward journey.

Ashwin glanced over, eyes bright. "This seems like we are keeping history."

I smiled. "Exactly."

Setting Up the Repo

We gathered around the screen. Manasa, who had taken the lead on Git setup, created the new repository.

```
$ git init

$ git remote add origin <repo_url>
```

Nikita added: "Let's make sure we document what each folder means and where this journey begins."

Akshay and Abhishek double-checked the file structure. We added a simple README.md, the Makefile, and our working code.

The First Commit

I typed:

$ git add.

$ git commit -m "Initial reference code: UART test, basic LED driver, and Makefile structure"

$ git push -u origin main

And it stood, our first commit. A time-stamped snapshot of ambition, collaboration, and all the late-night debugging we had already pushed through.

Marking the Moment

Jayalaxmi clapped softly. "I am happy," she expressed. "Like we've named our first child."

The situation appeared comical to us, but her assertion maintained truth. This is beyond code. That signified a promise, recorded in the version history. A point we could always return to. A baseline that would remind us of where we started, no matter how complex the project became.

"This is the start," I mentioned to the group. "Every feature, every bug fix, every lesson tracked, learned, improved. One commit at a time."

The Documentation Day

The codebase had grown into something massive, a breathing creature with hundreds of functions, macros, and modules. Newcomers looked at it like climbers staring at Everest.

"Alright," I said, standing by the whiteboard, marker in hand. "We've built drivers, debugged kernel panics, and even survived Akshay's '230 volts incident.' But there is something equally important that we have been ignoring."

Nikita raised an eyebrow. "Coffee breaks?"

I smiled. "Documentation." Not coffee breaks.

Groans filled the room. Manasa muttered, "Nobody reads that."

"True," "nobody reads bad documentation. But great documentation? That is the map that lets others walk the same path without falling into the same holes we did." I clicked through to the next slide on the projector. Big, bold letters: **DOXYGEN**.

This tool is not only for writing comments. It is about making our code self-explanatory. You put in your function descriptions, parameters, and return values in a structured way. Doxygen generates a full HTML or PDF reference for the entire project. It is like giving future engineers a GPS to navigate our work.

Without Doxygen

c Copy Edit

```c
int add_numbers(int a, int b) {
    return a + b;
}
```

What is wrong?

- No explanation of what the function does.
- No details about the parameters or return value.
- Anyone reading the code must figure it out themselves.

With Doxygen

```c
/**
 * @brief Adds two integers.
 *
 * This function takes two integer inputs, adds them,
 * and returns the sum.
 *
 * @param a First integer to add.
 * @param b Second integer to add.
 * @return Sum of the two integers.
 *
 * @note This function performs a simple addition;
 * it does not check for overflow.
 */
int add_numbers(int a, int b) {
    return a + b;
}
```

Why is it better:

- **@brief** gives a quick summary.
- **@param** explains each parameter.
- **@return** describes the return value.
- **@note** warns about a potential edge case.

When you run **Doxygen**, this comment turns into a clean, searchable HTML/PDF documentation page.

Ashwin grinned. “So basically… we write once, and Doxygen makes it look pretty?”

“Exactly,” “And when we are gone or when a new team takes over, this will be the thing that makes them say, ‘These folks knew what they were doing.’”

The room was quiet for a moment. Akshay, who usually dodged documentation like a cat dodges water, said. “Fine. But only if we can put my name in Comic Sans.”

We laughed, but by the end of the week, the first Doxygen build was live. For the first time, our code was not only functional; it was teachable.

Chapter Summary

Chapter 16: Track It. Save It. Share It. – The Power of Git and Doxygen

You wrote the code. You got rid of the bugs. You improved the design.

But what if something breaks tomorrow? How do you roll back? Collaborate? Review changes?

Chapter 16 of my **Technical Notes** introduces you to one of the most powerful tools in every developer’s arsenal:

Here is what you will learn:

- **Why Git Matters?**
  Track your changes, experiment safely, and collaborate with confidence.

- **Importance of a Repository**
  Centralise your work, manage branches, handle merges and make sure nothing ever gets lost.
- **Professional Grade Practices**
  Use commits, branches, pull requests, and logs to manage real-world embedded projects with team scale in mind.
- **Importance of Doxygen** – How automated documentation ensures clarity, maintainability, and smoother knowledge transfer in embedded projects.

Complete **Chapter 16. Practice using Git and Doxygen with purpose.**

Crafting superior code represents one aspect, and handling responsibly defines the characteristic of a superior engineer.

Good engineers write code. Great people never misplace that.

CHAPTER 17

AUTOMATE TO ELEVATE - BUILD SMARTER, DEPLOY FASTER

The Team They Did Not See Coming

We represented the still area on that level. The team without flashy titles, without senior architects. Only work.

Whenever someone walked past our bay, they barely paused. Some nodded, most did not. We were that team, the one pieced together with newcomers, interns, and the guy who once said, *"I'm not sure if I'm ready."*

In the manager's lounge, I overheard it once.

"They're just trying to keep them busy until something better comes along."

"I wouldn't bet a deadline on that group."

I said nothing.

In our bay, Akshay is debugging a SPI timing problem utilising a logic analyser naturally.

Ashwin had recently written his first device tree overlay, one he had studied all weekend to get right.

Manasa wrestled XML to UI integration for the app while sipping chilled coffee she left unfinished.

And Nikita? She guided them, silently confirming that each push moved things ahead, not only marking completion on Jira.

We did not speak much about the outside noise. We remained occupied with gaining knowledge. Too busy building.

The Curious Case of Appraisals

It started with a coffee break that turned into a full-blown interrogation.

Ashwin leaned across the table; his eyes narrowed in a teasing manner. Sateesh, you are being silent. Got any news for us?

I sipped gradually, buying time. "News like...?"

Akshay joined in, grinning. "You know what we mean. That magical word. The one that starts with A and ends with appraisal."

Even Nikita chimed in from behind her laptop. "We debugged code, built drivers, flashed boards, survived kernel panics… I trust we have earned something, haven't we?"

I laughed, putting up my hands. "Guys, I am not HR. I cannot wave a wand and increase your CTC."

"But", I continued, I can tell you this, your work has not gone unnoticed. The leadership is assessing our project outcome, and I ensured I highlighted your contributions.

Manasa raised an eyebrow. "So, we'll likely hear something... soon-ish?"

I smiled. "Sooner than soon-ish. At the same time, let us continue doing what we do best, building what others view as unachievable."

The mood lightened. Abhishek clapped his hands with emotion. "Fine. We will hold off our protest march… for now."

Appraisals may be a mystery, but team spirit. That was alive and thriving.

Automate or Stagnate: The Turning Point in Our Build Process

It started with a sigh.

Each time we required a fresh build, someone needed to clean, configure, compile, flash manually, and hope that nothing broke in the middle. Ashwin, at one time, spent one day debugging a build error only to realise someone forgot a make clean. It was not laziness. It was **inefficiency**.

One evening, as the team packed up, I stayed behind, staring at the terminal logs. The build has grown. Codebase complexity was rising, and we could not afford to lose precious hours chasing typos or missing steps.

"We need to automate this," I whispered to myself.

The next morning, I gathered everyone.

"Team, it is time we let go of manual build chaos. We are not just writing code; we are building a product. And automation is our foundation for scale."

Nikita nodded. "But what exactly should we automate?"

"Everything we can," I replied. "Build scripts, environment setup, versioning, post-build tests. Our process should be repeatable, fast, and reliable."

Why Automation Matters?

I wrote that on the whiteboard.

- **Consistency** – same build every time, for everyone.
- **Speed** – no more repeated manual steps.
- **Early Error Detection** – Automate test cases post-build.
- **Environment Setup** – Same dependencies, same versions, everywhere.
- **Scalability** – one-click builds work even as the project grows.

Abhishek mentioned that this will let new team members begin sooner as well.

We wrote our first **build.sh** script. The system cleaned outdated documents, set up the proper toolchain, executed make, and logs got pushed into a report. Eventually, we planned to integrate a Git hook for auto-builds on every commit.

And just like that, we turned our messy build ritual into a structured routine.

From Code to Confidence: Building Our First CI/CD Pipeline

The team had grown. So had our codebase.

Every merge, every feature branch, every last-minute hot fix came with its own uncertainty. Did it break the build? Did we miss a test? Would it even boot on the board?

We built quicker than we verified.

One late evening, as I was pushing a bug fix and hoping I had not broken something else, the realisation struck me:

We have reached a point where we cannot rely on hope. Confidence is necessary. CI/CD is a necessity for us.

The next morning, I called for a short huddle.

"Team, we are doing great. But our workflow ends with the last commit. We need to go one step further, automated testing, build triggers, and deployment checks. We need a CI/CD pipeline."

Manasa, sipping her coffee, asked, "CI/CD sounds fancy, but where do we start?"

"From where it hurts," I smiled. The pain points: manual builds, missing regressions, forgotten tests, late-night patch merges.

The Setup Begins

We started small. A Git commit triggered a build script using GitHub Actions. We integrated unit tests to validate the HAL and application logic. Instantly, the system sent the team errors by email. No more surprises.

Akshay added build badge status to the README.

From CI to CD

Once confident with **Continuous Integration**, we ventured into **Continuous Deployment**.

If a commit passed all tests on main, it would automatically push the firmware image to the OTA server and notify the QA team.

And best of all, they flashed demo boards overnight. By morning, the devices were ready for testing.

Jayalaxmi beamed, "Now that's magic!"

Beyond the tools, it was a mindset shift.

No more untested code. No more broken builds during demo week. We trusted the system, and the system worked because we built it right.

"CI/CD didn't just automate our pipeline,". "It automated our **trust**."

Chapter Summary

Chapter 17: Automate to Elevate – Build Smarter, Deploy Faster

You wrote the code. You tested it. However, if you still construct and deploy by hand, you are holding back the strength of genuine engineering efficiency.

Chapter 17 of my **Technical Notes** focuses on taking your workflow to the next level with **automation and continuous integration.**

Here is what you will explore:

- **Importance of Build Automation**
  Eliminate repetitive tasks. Ensure consistent builds. Reduce human error. Automate with tools like Make, CMake, and scripting.
- **Importance of Continuous Integration (CI)**
  Execute tests, lint checks, and builds each time code gets pushed. Keep your project stable and team productive.
- **Importance of Continuous Deployment (CD)**
  Deploy updates to test or live settings with ease. Which accelerates release rhythms and receives genuine input quickly.

Complete Chapter 17. Learn the tools. Set up pipelines.

As in modern times, people consider fast and reliable shipping necessary, not optional.

Code that ships itself is code that wins.

CHAPTER 18

TEST LIKE A PRO - FROM FUNCTIONS TO FULL SYSTEMS

Testing the Core: Building Trust, One Case at a Time

The CI/CD pipeline was live, humming quietly in the background like a silent guardian. But even the strongest chain fails if the weakest link goes unchecked.

That weak link? **Testing.**

We had automation; we had builds. But did we have *confidence* in the code itself?

One morning during our daily stand-up, I asked the team:

"Can you say with certainty that yesterday's commit broke nothing?"

The silence answered for them.

So, I wrote on the board:

Unit Testing. System Testing. Regression Testing.

"We're not just writing code anymore," "We're writing promises, and we need tests to hold us accountable."

Ashwin and Akshay started with **unit tests**. A simple C framework wrapped every HAL function, GPIO, I2C, and SPI with test cases.

Manasa created a test interface in the app to simulate sensor inputs and verify edge behaviours.

Nikita took it further, writing test scripts to run on actual boards.

- Boot tests.
- Peripheral initialisation checks.
- Communication interface validation.
- Real-time sensor feedback loops.

The CI pipeline logged failures, analysed them, and reported them to GitHub.

We made every bug we fixed into a regression test.

"If it failed once," I told them, "It can fail again. Let us make sure it never does."

Nikita organised the regression suite. Nikita documented each test, linked each to its original bug ID, and added each to nightly builds.

The code grew, but now with guardrails.

Fear turned into **curiosity**.

Doubt transformed into **confidence**.

We were no longer hoping things worked.

We **knew** they did.

"Testing doesn't slow us down," I told the team over coffee. "It's the reason we can move faster." Everyone nodded.

Chapter Summary

Chapter 18: Test Like a Pro – From Functions to Full Systems

Writing code is only half the journey. The actual difficulty is making sure the system runs dependably, remains firm, and unifies smoothly without damaging anything different.

Chapter 18 of my **Technical Notes** focuses on a critical discipline that separates amateurs from professionals:

Here is what you will cover:

- **Unit Testing**
  Test each function, module, or component in isolation. Catch bugs early. Build confidence as you go.
- **System Testing**
  Validate the entire integrated system. Simulate real-world conditions and make sure all modules work in harmony.
- **Regression Testing**
  Ensure today's updates do not break yesterday's features. Make automated. Make it a habit.

Complete Chapter 18. Make testing part of your development DNA.

Since testing is not a phase, this represents a mindset.

CHAPTER 19

WHAT DID YOU MISS? - THE POWER OF CODE COVERAGE WITH GCOV

Reading Between the Lines: Unlocking Code Coverage with gcov

The builds operated. The test achieved the desired outcome. But as I leaned back in my chair one evening, I asked myself a quiet question:

What if there's code we have never even touched?

That night, I scribbled a word in my notebook:

gcov — *GNU coverage analysis tool.*

I walked into the lab the next day, and the team buzzed around the dev boards.

"Guys, we've written tests. But how do we know they are enough?"

Akshay blinked.

Ashwin paused mid-keystroke.

Manasa raised an eyebrow.

Nikita leaned in.

"We're introducing code coverage today," "With gcov."

We recompiled our firmware with -fprofile-arcs -ftest-coverage. The build spat out .gcno and .gcda files, strange at first, but golden once decoded.

One line after another, we could see which portions of our code experienced testing… and which existed as ghosts in the machine.

Manasa exclaimed,

"We missed testing the error path in the I2C driver!"

Astonishingly, even Nikita seemed shocked.

"Our init code for SPI has a branch that never got hit."

We visualised coverage with lcov, creating colourful HTML reports.

Green meant tested.

Red meant danger.

After integrating gcov, our coverage reports became our daily checkpoints, bright green where we tested thoroughly, ominous red where logic remained untouched.

One module stood out like a sore thumb: **Sensor Communication**.

Despite the tests, the coverage sat at **63%**.

"Why is this so low?" Ashwin asked, frowning at the report.

"Because", I replied, "real-world bugs do not always live on the happy path. They lurk in the edge cases."

We split the module into paths, initialisation, timeout handling, corrupted data, and retry loops.

Each team member took ownership of their module's coverage.

Manasa wrote tests that mimicked incomplete or garbage sensor data. The parser should reject them, but we saw it crash instead.

"Why would a null byte cause that?" she muttered, tracing the logic.

Boom **off-by-one** bug. Fixed. Test added.

Akshay simulated delayed I2C responses and analysed the retry logic.

"Hey, this loop retries 3 times, but what if the first success comes late on the third attempt?"

The coverage showed we never hit that last chance success path. A fresh test came into being.

Ashwin found a logic branch that activated only when two conditions failed simultaneously. It had not triggered once in hundreds of test runs.

He crafted a test where power brownouts and sensor noise occurred together.

"Edge cases are like rare bugs in production," he said. "Unlikely doesn't mean impossible."

Over the next few days, our reports evolved:

- 63% → 77%
- 77% → 89%
- 89% → 93%

But more than the numbers, the code felt stronger.

No longer chasing bugs, we hunted weaknesses.

I looked at the glowing screen of our final report.

"Every red line we turned green… might have been a crash waiting to happen."

The team smiled. Not just engineers, now we were guardians of reliability.

afternoon, our boss dropped by.

"I heard you've got a new testing metric?"

We showed him the reports. A crisp 93% overall coverage.

He smiled.

"Numbers speak. This is good work."

Coverage was not about hitting 100%. Grasping our code thoroughly counted. About knowing what we *could* trust, and what still lurked in the shadows.

Chapter Summary

Chapter 19: What Did You Miss? – The Power of Code Coverage with gcov

You have written tests. You think your code is solid.

But how much of it is being tested?

Chapter 19 of my **Technical Notes** dives into **code coverage analysis** because untested code is **untamed code**.

Here is what you will discover:

- **Importance of Coverage with** gcov
  Find out exactly which lines of code are being executed during tests and which ones are not.
- **Why Coverage Matters?**
  Improve test quality. Identify the dead code. Increase confidence before deployment.
- **Read Coverage Reports Like a Pro**
  Use gcov to highlight weak spots and strengthen your codebase one line at a time.

Complete Chapter 19. Measure your tests. Close the gaps.

Because good engineers write code, but **great engineers test all of it.**

If you do not measure coverage, you are only guessing. And guessing has no place in production.

CHAPTER 20

LET THE SYSTEM WORK FOR YOU - MASTERING CRON JOBS AND UDEV

The Day We Stopped Guessing USB Ports

It was one of those mornings where every table in the lab looked like an electronics scrapyard, with cables coiled like snakes, boards stacked like pancakes, and laptops tethered to more devices than they could handle.

Akshay plugged in the new debug board, looked at the terminal, and frowned.

"Which one is it this time? /dev/ttyUSB0 or /dev/ttyUSB7?"

Nikita was already scrolling through the dmesg output. "No idea… maybe this one? Or… nope. Permission denied."

We had been here before. Every time someone re-plugged a device, the name changed. Scripts broke, test cases failed, and tempers flared.

That is when I called everyone over.

"Alright, gather up. Today, we stop chasing device names. We are going to use udev."

I explained:

"udev is the device manager for Linux. It listens when hardware appears, and we can tell it exactly how to name and configure our devices no more guessing. We write a rule, match by the device's serial number or vendor ID, and boom, our board will always appear as /dev/our_board."

Nikita grinned. "So, no more changing my script every time it is /dev/ttyUSB3?"

"Absolutely," "Consistency, automation, and no more 'Where is my port?' drama."

By the end of the day, every board in the lab had a permanent, human-readable name. Our scripts ran without modification, and the room felt… calmer.

Sometimes, progress is not about writing more code it is about making sure your tools work for you, not against you.

The Clock That Never Sleeps: Understanding the Power of Cron Jobs

It was late evening. The team had mostly gone home, but I stayed behind, desk-bound, observing the logs move on the terminal. That is when I realised someone had not saved the logs for three days.

"Wait… wasn't that supposed to be automated?" I muttered.

Turns out, the script existed, but no one had set it to run automatically. That night, we learned a valuable lesson, and it started with introducing the team to something deceptively simple but incredibly powerful: the **cron job**.

Morning Stand-Up:

"Alright, team," I began, "have you ever wished your system could run tasks on its own, at midnight, or every Monday, or even every minute?"

Akshay raised his hand.

"Like auto-cleaning logs?"

Ashwin nodded.

"Or restarting services if they crash?"

"Exactly," "Enter ***cron,*** your system's built-in scheduler. It never forgets, never sleeps, and never complains."

Where Cron Changed Everything

- **Daily Backups:**
  Manasa wrote a script to back up log files every day at 12 AM. Now, no one has to worry about lost logs again.

- **Health Checks:**
  Nikita scheduled a watchdog script to check for stuck processes every hour, auto-restarting them if needed.

- **Resource Monitoring:**
  Akshay created a cron job to log CPU and memory usage every 10 minutes into a CSV file for later analysis.

- **Sensor Calibration Reminder:**
  Ashwin added a weekly reminder to calibrate external sensors, pinging the team via email every Monday morning.

Why It Mattered?

1. **Automation Consistency**
   Humans forget. Machines do not. Cron gave our project reliability.
2. **Offloading Routine Work**
   Instead of wasting time on repetitive tasks, we let cron handle them and focused on more important engineering problems.

3. **Better Debugging**
   With consistent log backups and system monitoring, tracing bugs became much easier.
4. **Resilience**
   Some cron jobs acted like safety nets, watchdogs, restarters, and disk space monitors saved us from potential failures.

By the end of the week, our project was no longer just "functional."

It was **alive and self-aware**, thanks to cron.

"Now," I told the team, "if someone asks who's running night shifts around here, tell them cron's got it covered."

Chapter Summary

Chapter 20: Let the System Work for You – Mastering Cron Jobs and Udev

You wrote the code. You tested the system.

But can your program run itself at 12 a.m. on Sunday without you being there?

Chapter 20 of my **Technical Notes** is all about **automating repetitive tasks** using one of Linux's most powerful scheduling tools: **cron** and **udev**

Here is what you will learn:

- **Importance of Cron Jobs**
  Automate backups, logs, cleanups, script execution, system monitoring and more.

- **Real-World Use Cases**
  Schedule hardware diagnostics, firmware updates, or data uploads without lifting a finger.
- **Write, Schedule, and Manage Your Own Cron Jobs**
  Learn how to use cron, including how to schedule tasks and the best ways to do it.
- **Importance of Udev** – Dynamic device management in Linux, crucial for handling peripherals, automating rules, and enabling hardware-software interaction seamlessly.

Complete Chapter 20. Start automating tasks.

Because smart engineers do not just build systems that work, they build systems that **work on their own.**

Automation is not the future. It is the standard.

THE GRAND UNVEIL - WHERE EFFORT MEETS RECOGNITION

Trial by Fire: Time to Test the Complete Setup

The sun had just climbed above the horizon when I walked into the lab, coffee in hand, heart racing with a mix of anticipation and pride. Today turned into not just another workday, it is the day. The boards got wired; the software got flashed; the sensors got calibrated; and the logs stood ready to capture every heartbeat of the system.

Our complete setup stood before us like a machine ready to breathe.

I gathered the team, Nikita with her ever-sharp eye for anomalies, Akshay and Ashwin, who had grown from curious beginners to confident microcontroller hands, Manasa with her steady grip on the Android front, and Akshay monitoring the data flow. Ashwin finished validating the setup files again.

"Alright, team," I said, drawing in a breath. "It is time. We built, we learned, we fixed, and we waited. Let us test the complete setup."

One by one, we powered up each module. LEDs blinked in rhythm, sensors started feeding data to the console, the app came alive on the tablet, and the message logs began to grow.

There were hiccups, of course. A dangling GPIO pin here, a misaligned serial baud rate there. But now, we remained unfazed. We stood prepared.

Manasa shouted from the far desk, "Data is coming in smoothly. Apps synced!"

Nikita chimed in, " Message Broker works perfectly. No dropouts!"

I watched the console with a quiet smile. It is not only testing it equals evidence. Proof of teamwork, late nights, burnt boards, tough bugs, and unwavering grit.

"Team," I mentioned, "we are not simply testing hardware. We are seeing the result of every bit of effort we poured in.

A few more tweaks, a couple of retests, and the entire setup ran flawlessly for the next hour.

When we paused at last, laughter, high-fives, and a silent understanding existed between us.

We had crossed another milestone. Together.

Between the Lab and the Hospital Ward

Release day requires unwavering focus and precision; you cannot look away from the screen until everything is perfect.

However, this time, the stress seemed different.

My phone kept lighting up with updates from the hospital. My father was in surgery for a high-risk procedure on his heart. I wanted nothing more than to be there holding my family's hands, waiting outside the operating theatre. Instead, I was in the office, hands on the keyboard, eyes on the release dashboard, leading my team through the final integration steps.

Every commit pushed felt like a bead of sweat rolling down my back. Each delay made me anxious, not only for the project, but because time was passing in the hospital while I was away.

Colleagues could see it on my face the conflict, the weight.

"Go, we'll manage," someone whispered.

But the truth was, both places needed me. The release had dependencies that only I could resolve. The hospital had a patient who was my father.

So, I split myself in half. One half were in the war room checking logs, resolving merge conflicts, and running last-minute tests. One side of my mind prayed, counted the minutes, and imagined the doctor's voice saying, "He is safe."

When the final build passed and the release email went out, I exhaled for the first time that day. I did not wait for the applause or the wrap-up meeting. I grabbed my bag and ran.

Hours later, I stood by my father's bed, the hum of the monitors oddly like the hum of the server room.

That day taught me something no process document ever will. The leadership is not about being everywhere at once and is not about choosing between work and life. Sometimes it is about carrying both until they are all right. It is about standing where you are most needed, trusting the rest to hold until you get there.

Reflection:

That day reminded me that engineering is not just about code, tools, or deadlines; it is about responsibility. In embedded systems, when a product ships, it becomes part of someone's life. Debugging through fatigue, double-checking configurations under pressure, these are not just technical skills; they are acts of care.

The Clash with QA: Your Code is Broken!

The first build was finally ready. After long nights of coding, debugging, and integrating modules, we handed it over to the testing team. We expected issues, of course; that is what testing is for, but we were not ready for the storm that followed.

Within hours, the bug reports began pouring in.

"Feature X crashes after three inputs."

"System freezes if you reset it twice."

"Communication protocol fails at random."

By the next day, the testing lab sounded like a courtroom.

"This code isn't production-ready!" one tester shouted.

"Your test cases are unrealistic!" a developer fired back.

"It's not our fault you didn't handle edge cases."

"And it's not our job to fix your test environment!"

The air grew heavy with accusations. Developers felt attacked. Testers perceived neglect. Every bug appeared to be a personal slight, and every defence sounded like an excuse.

Finally, Boss stepped in.

"Stop. We are not enemies here," he said firmly. "The customer does not care if it is a dev bug or a QA oversight. They only care if it works."

The silence that followed was hard but necessary. Slowly, we reset the tone: developers sat with testers, walking through logs together. Testers explained their scenarios; developers explained the code paths. We stopped saying **"your fault"** and started saying **"what's the fix?"**

By the end of the week, we had fewer arguments, cleaner builds, and, ironically, the strongest respect between teams. Because nothing builds trust like surviving a fight together.

Showtime: Presenting the Tested Setup to the Boss

The lab air felt thick with quiet excitement. Screens glowed softly, sensor readings streamed steadily, and the faint hum of the boards signalled all existed and stood ready.

The clock read 11:00 AM. The boss had scheduled a walk-through of our tested setup. This signified the instant we had been constructing toward for months. Our systems communicated. Data flowed. We had slain bugs. This remained our success to share.

I quickly gathered the team. Nikita ran one last check on the message queue. Akshay and Ashwin verified the board voltages and confirmed all processes are up and stable. Manasa swiped through the Android app's dashboard one final time, ensuring the UI displayed the sensor data in real-time. Abhishek stood by with the logs and analysis reports.

The door creaked open, and in walked the boss.

"Hello everyone! Whispers reached me concerning your creation. I cannot wait to witness it in action.

I am very excited to see the development and what you have prepared for the demonstration.

I nodded. "Yes, sir. End-to-end functionality. All modules up and running."

We walked him through the setup step by step. Nikita explained the data flow and how we used Message Broker for communication. Akshay showcased the sensor calibration and real-time readings. Ashwin demonstrated the power of sequencing and error handling. Manasa flipped the tablet screen toward him, displaying smooth graphs, alerts, and controls. I spoke about the hard work for the system: building, debugging, flashing, examination and failing before triumphing.

The Boss stayed silent for some time. A slight smile appeared on his face.

"Impressive," he said. "Clean, stable, and well-coordinated. I understand how much you've all put into this. Good job."

I looked at my team. Their eyes lit up not only from the praise but from the recognition. We had crossed from planning to execution. From doubt to deliver.

As the boss walked out, he added, "Prepare for the next phase. This signified the opening phase.

We looked at one another, tired, proud, and ready.

Countdown to Deployment: Gearing Up for the Real World

The room remained energised after the boss's visit. The recognition seemed earned, but everyone knew it was not a time to relax, not yet. Assuming that the demo is our dress rehearsal, deployment becomes the main stage. And the world would not be as forgiving as our lab.

I gathered the team for a quick huddle.

"Great job, everyone," I began. "But now it is time to think bigger. This setup needs to survive outside these walls. We deploy next week."

Nikita leaned in. "Let us list everything that can go wrong. Network drops, power failures, corrupted logs…"

"... hardware resets, memory overflows, unexpected sensor behaviour," Akshay added, scribbling into a notepad.

Ashwin chimed in, "Let us simulate a field power cut. I will monitor boot recovery."

Manasa nodded. "I'll check for data loss scenarios on the app side and add offline caching."

We began building redundancy into our system. Automatic restarts, watchdog timers, and local buffering. Components were stress-tested by us. We exposed them to noisy inputs as well as random shutdowns. Low-signal conditions were mimicked by us. Slowly, we built not just a project but a *resilient system.*

Meanwhile, Abhishek and Jayalaxmi helped in preparing the deployment checklist. Firmware versions, backups, rollback strategies, and logging mechanisms got double-checked.

"Every detail matters," I reminded the team. "Deployment doesn't forgive assumptions."

By the end of the week, we had not just fixed bugs we had fortified the entire structure. What once existed as a tangle of tests and hopeful commands is now a disciplined, production-ready flow.

As we looked at the devices humming steadily, I felt a strange sense of calm. We are all set. And this time, the world would see it too.

The Day It Goes Live

As I came to the office, the sun peeked over the horizon, but I was not first. The team had already assembled laptops open, terminals glowing, coffee cups half-full. That day was for deployment.

"Today, our work leaves the lab," I said, breaking the early silence. "Let's make sure it lands well."

Nikita had double-checked the deployment scripts. Akshay and Ashwin synced the newest software to USB sticks and OTA bundles. Manasa is testing the app's live data stream a final time. Each group participant shifted quietly, intently, we all knew this was not a trial.

By 10 AM, we arrived at the client site, boards and tools packed in padded cases. As we unpacked and started connecting the devices, a quiet hum filled the room: fans spinning, LEDs blinking, the comforting signs of a system coming to life.

One board blinked erratically. Ashwin and Akshay exchanged a glance. Without a word, they rebooted, checked serial logs, and re-flashed the firmware. In minutes, it turned stable.

Meanwhile, Manasa affirmed that the app received sensor data in real time. “No lag, no drops,” she said with a smile.

The client watched with curiosity, occasionally asking questions. I explained the architecture, the fallback mechanisms, and the OTA upgrade paths. For each query, we possessed not only a response but proof, stats, and illustrations.

By 2 PM, all devices were live and stable. Logs streamed. Dashboards lit up. We ran a few controlled stress tests on-site, and the system held strong.

After that, silence arrived.

Not the anxious kind. The sort where all operate properly.

I glanced at the team, dust on our sleeves, smudges on our fingers, but eyes full of pride.

“It’s live,” I said quietly. “We did it.”

That evening, back at the office, we did not rush home. We sat together in the cafeteria as a team, not as individuals; we had shipped something real, something that would now exist outside of us, doing what it is built to do.

And that feeling… meant everything.

The Unexpected Ping

It had only been two days since deployment. The system was stable, data was flowing, and logs were clean. Everything had gone smoother than we expected, almost too smooth.

That is when I saw the email.

Subject: *Sensor Module 3 – Data Inconsistency Observed*

I paused. The client had seen that one board, Sensor Module 3, was reporting irregular temperature values. Occasionally, it would spike to 127°C for a split second before returning to normal. An obvious outlier, but why?

I gathered the team in our war-room corner.

"Alright," projecting the log graphs. "Do you spot those spikes?" Let us isolate them.

Akshay pulled up the raw data. Ashwin began checking the board's analogue-to-digital conversion logic. Manasa confirmed the app was not misrendering; what it received was exactly what the backend had logged.

"That 127... looks like an overflow," Nikita muttered. "Could be an uninitialized variable or noise not filtered."

We hooked up a CRO to a test board and simulated similar input. Sure enough, under certain startup conditions, the sensor module was initialised with garbage values before calibration kicked in.

"That's our bug," I said, exhaling. "We missed the delay before the sensor stabilises. It is not a hardware fault; it is timing."

We patched the firmware with a proper warm-up delay and added a sanity check to ignore improbable spikes. A quick OTA update pushed the fix live.

By evening, the client confirmed, "All clear now. Readings seem consistent. Thanks for the quick response!"

I looked around at the team, no panic, no blame, just focused minds solving real problems. This was more than code or circuits. This was ownership.

We did not just deploy software. We deployed accountability.

And the Team Award Goes To...

The crowd packed the room. People from every department stood shoulder to shoulder, murmuring, sipping coffee, pretending not to be nervous. It was that time of the quarter, the **Team Excellence Award** announcement.

Our team stood near the back. No matching t-shirts. No over-the-top cheering. Only calm assurance, smirks passed as hushed high-fives. We went through fire night builds, unexpected bugs, and last-minute client requests. But we delivered. On time. Every time.

The HR head, Ms Kavita, walked to the mic. Behind her, the screen displayed the words:

"TEAM EXCELLENCE AWARD OF THE YEAR,"

She smiled and looked around. "Every team here has worked hard this year. However, one group distinguished itself not only for their skills but also for their character, cooperation, and determined accountability.

People shuffled, eyebrows lifted.

That is when our boss, Mr Raghav, stepped forward and took the mic.

He cleared his throat. "This team did not ask for attention. They took no time in waiting for instructions. They anticipated problems and fixed them before they became blockers. When others slowed down, they took up the responsibility. After pushing, failing, and learning, the team delivered a solution, and the company is now showcasing it.

Silence.

"And so… this year, the **Team Excellence Award** goes to…"

He paused.

"The Embedded Systems and Platform Team!"

It took a moment to register.

Following cheers. Applause. Claps that grew louder as people turned to look at us, surprised, some stunned, a few nodding as if to say, "Finally."

Our team lead gave us the nod — *go.* We made our way to the front. Not marching. Only... moving as a unit, who toughed it out and emerged better.

Raghav shook hands. Kavita handed us the trophy. Flashbulbs popped. Someone shouted, "Speech!" but we did not need one.

One of us held the trophy high.

Team Celebration

Within minutes, the entire bay buzzed. Nikita spun her chair toward me, mock-serious: "Well, Mr Project Lead, when's the party?"

I looked around.

"Alright," I said, standing up, "let's go make this memory count."

No whiteboards, no bug lists, no device logs, only laughter, clinking glasses of soda and coffee, and the warm chatter of a group that had battled together. We found ourselves at the same cafe near the office, the one we used to escape to when pressure felt too heavy.

The jokes flowed easily.

"Ashwin, remember when you connected VCC to ground and smoked that sensor?"

"That was 'intentional stress testing,' thank you very much!"

We laughed until our stomachs hurt. Nikita mock-rolled her eyes as we teased her about being the "walking debugger." Manasa finally confessed she once Googled "What is UART?" and pretended to know already.

I watched them. The team I once needed to guide through the basics is now discussing optimisations and production strategies like pros. That was the actual festivity, not the treats, not the funny stories, but the voyage we gained.

Before we left, Jayalaxmi raised her cup.

"To us and to the guy who led us here."

They all looked at me. I gave a smile, sensing small, uttering only a statement:

"To all of us because no one builds something great alone."

None of this would have been possible without all of you.

Nikita, whose sharp insights and unwavering expertise, helped us untangle problems before they became roadblocks. You were our anchor, our silent strength.

Akshay and **Ashwin**, who dived headfirst into the world of microcontrollers, were curious, relentless, and never afraid to ask the right questions. Your growth was inspiring.

Manasa, who embraced the challenge of unfamiliar tools and technologies, turned confusion into confident execution. Your dedication shone through.

Abhishek and **Jayalaxmi**, who stood by, contributed with energy and humour when we needed it the most. You made us remember that fantastic teams do not only work relentlessly, but they also savour the experience as a group.

Every late night, every debugging session, every laugh over burnt boards or a failed build, it all mattered. It all added up to this moment of success.

So, from the bottom of my heart, **thank you**. Not only for the work, but for trusting the vision, in the process and in me.

"Hey Sateesh," Akshay started, his voice unusually soft. "We only wanted to mention... thank you."

I blinked. "For what?"

Nikita chimed in, "For everything. We thank you for having faith in us when we lacked faith in ourselves.

Ashwin stated, "You never gave us the impression that we were lesser, even when we goofed with microcontrollers."

Manasa smiled. "You guided me through Android and web development when all I had was curiosity and a hundred doubts."

"You never gave up on us," Abhishek said. "Even when the boards burned, when code crashed, when things didn't work, you stood by us."

Jayalaxmi, with a little emotion in her voice, said, "You headed not only the project." You gave us the sense that we belonged to something meaningful; something we possessed as well.

I was stunned and humbled.

I had always put faith in empowering people, in trusting them enough so they could rise higher than they thought possible. They stood here, developed in skills, confidence, and clarity, not only teammates, but builders in every sense.

"You believed in us," Akshay repeated. "And that changed everything."

In a flash, the burden of each night spent, each diagram on a whiteboard, each tolerant explanation… it all appeared worthwhile.

I did not speak much; I smiled and nodded. But I could perceive it within me.

This was a real success.

Beyond finishing the project.

But seeing your team shine.

The Day the Spotlight Shifted

That morning, the conference room appeared quite bright, not because of the lights, but the energy.

We had been called in without a brief explanation. Just a meeting invite from the boss.

Subject: Project Wrap-Up & Special Announcement.

I considered it to be a retrospective. Maybe a checklist for the next phase. Upon our entering, the table displayed little, classy boxes each bearing a name tag.

The boss stood at the front, arms crossed but smiling.

"You built not only a solution," he began, you built trust. Across platforms, yes, though more significantly, with each other. That merits a greater than a 'well done' email.

He nodded to HR. The lights dimmed just a bit, and a slide appeared.

"Recognition Ceremony – Project Phoenix,"

Names got announced, one by one.

"**Nikita** – for never giving up during kernel panic hell. Your perseverance kept our boards alive."

"**Akshay** – for debugging without sleep and documenting without being asked. You lit more than LEDs, you lit a path for others."

"**Manasa** – in making the Android app, you acted as our hidden backbone."

"**Ashwin** – for asking the right questions at the right time. You saved us from going in circles more times than I can count."

And after that, he looked toward me.

"And **Sateesh**… for leading without ego, teaching without tiring, and having faith in this team from day one."

The applause that came after did not seem like noise. It seemed like belonging.

As we handed out prizes, shared embarrassed looks and pleased smiles, it seemed obvious this was not only about honours.

It involved getting noticed.

Being valued.

And most of all… being a team.

The Numbers That Spoke

Usual morning, the system pinged; the subject line made everyone pause mid-sip of coffee.

"Appraisal Letters,"

Silence… followed by a scramble.

Akshay checked before anyone else. His eyes widened.

"Nikita… I believe I am seeing things. This… this is good. Very good.

She rushed over, peeking at his screen before checking her own.

"No way… this cannot be right. Did we all get this?"

One by one, the team checked. One by one, the quiet grew radiant, and later cries.

Everyone had received strong appraisals. Not only regular increases but actual recognition.

Tears welled in Manasa's eyes.

I viewed them from the bay's other side, my group, previously doubtful, previously inexperienced with anchored systems. At present, they are celebrating not solely for themselves, but for each other.

Since it concerned more than figures in some text. This involved proof.

Someone proved that growth has consequences.

The endeavour matters.

Trusting people works.

And now, our bay did not feel like only a workspace.

It appeared as a little cosmos where each recent evening, each issue resolved, each supportive act... finally gave compensation.

What Next?

The celebration mellowed, leaving behind half-empty coffee cups, the hum of tired laptops, and glowing faces still smiling from the day's big news.

We sat together in our small part of the workplace, no longer a team grouped over bugs and boards, but a unit that went through something.

Akshay leaned back, arms crossed, with a thoughtful look on his face.

"You know… this appraisal was more than I expected. But also, it made me realise how far we have come."

Ashwin nodded. "Remember when we were arguing over GPIO pinmux? Now we are optimising driver code and pushing patches like pros."

Manasa added, "We built our own toolchain, brought up custom boards, and debugged in live conditions. This level of growth, I believe, was unexpected by all of us.

Listening quietly, a smile appeared on my face. I finally voiced the question that had been on my mind all day.

"So… what next?"

The room was still.

Nikita broke the silence, voice confident.

"I want to contribute to upstream Linux. Maybe start with device tree bindings or driver submissions."

Akshay grinned. "RTOS performance tuning. That is my next rabbit hole."

Ashwin: "I will write a blog series. Teach others what we have learned the hard way."

Manasa: "And I want to lead a sub-team. Train the interns. Give back what someone gave me. "

I glanced about, heart swelling not only with pride, but with something rarer: certainty.

They were not simply dreaming. They meant it.

The project concluded, but their story newly unfolds.

Growth is not a destination; it is a mindset.

We only began.

The Words That Stayed With Me

I was verifying the concluding paperwork as a notification appeared on the display.

"Can you drop by my cabin for a minute?"

– Boss

I took a deep breath, stood up, and walked toward his cabin. My mind raced. Did we miss something? Did a problem arise during quality analysis?

I knocked. He looked up, smiled, and waved me in.

"Close the door," he said.

I sat down, still unsure of what to expect.

He looked up from the final report, flipping the last page shut. His eyes did not carry the usual urgency of deadlines or checklists. This time, something else existed behind them, something rarer.

He stood, walked around his desk, and said, "Sateesh, you've done something incredible here." Leading this project was not all you did. You have established a team. You revealed hidden strengths in people, which they did not realise existed. "The way you handled the pressure was great." The way you handled setbacks.

You created a team without resources, guided them through challenges, setbacks, and even stressful crises. You pulled long nights, debugged the impossible, and kept your team encouraged. It is not simple. It embodies leadership.

He extended his hand. I shook it, firm but humbled.

"For every late night, every moment you doubted yourself and still pushed forward, well done. I saw it all. You earned this."

"Thank you, sir," I said. "For trusting me when I did not even trust myself. The faith created a contrast.

Sir, this was not only in connection with accomplishing a task. It was about demonstrating what belief, consistency, and a little courage could build. The contribution is not solely mine. That group grew together as a unit.

He smiled. "It's precisely the reason I considered you a suitable individual."

Stepping from the room, his statements resounded within me not merely as flattery but as a journey's echo. Every difficulty, the long evenings, the doubt they had moulded not only the project, but the individual I was evolving into.

Occasionally, one instance of gratefulness will be sufficient to support you through many further instances.

COMING IN THE NEXT EDITION – THE JOURNEY CONTINUES

Sparks have flown from our first LED, as you have seen.

The tension of midnight kernel panics is something you have experienced.

You have witnessed our team's struggles, battles, and triumphs.

But the real adventure?

We have only just powered it on.

In the **next revision**, we will push deeper into the heart of embedded systems where speed, security, and innovation collide:

- **Security in Embedded Systems** – From secure boot to encrypted firmware updates, we will lock down devices against the unseen threats of tomorrow.
- **Passing the Test** – Compliance & Certifications.
- **Power Mastery** - Ensure that every milliamp is extracted from a battery until the device outlasts the problem it was created to solve.
- **Over-the-Air (OTA) Updates** – Shipping fixes and features to thousands of devices without touching a single one in person.
- **Real-Time Debugging** – Peering inside a running system without pausing its heartbeat.

- **Advanced Networking Protocols** – Teaching devices to talk smarter, faster, and with purpose.
- **AI at the Edge** – Providing microcontrollers the ability to process, predict, and adapt.
- **Factory Floor** – Manufacturing & Production.

In each chapter, you will find not just how we crafted these solutions, but the experience of fighting for them when the stakes were high, the deadlines close, and the boards stubborn.

So, turn the last page knowing this: **our story is not over**.

The coming version will take you further, faster, and deeper than you imagined possible.

Because in embedded systems, as in life, there is always another level to unlock.

A NOTE TO THE ASPIRING ENGINEERS

Dear Reader,

What you have read is not just a collection of stories; it is a lived experience, shaped by challenges, failures, growth, and resilience.

I invite you to explore the **technical notes**. These are not simply papers; these are stepping stones. They reflect the exact knowledge, practices, and insights that helped me transform from a struggling beginner into a confident embedded engineer.

You do not need to be a genius to become a great embedded engineer.

You simply require discipline, curiosity, and a roadmap. This is the roadmap. Adhere to it, and you will not only construct projects you will construct your career.

Whether you are a student, a new engineer, or someone seeking clarity in this vast field, **my notes are your map**, and my path is one you can walk too.

Follow the flow. Practice consistently. Do not simply read, try, break, fix, and build.

Success does not arrive overnight. But if you stay curious, stay patient, and stay hungry, you will get there and may even go further.

Your journey is waiting. Make it count.

Staying Connected

This book is just the beginning.

My technical notes support many of the concepts, examples, and deep-dive explanations you will encounter here. They are a curated set of documents, code snippets, schematics, and practice exercises designed to help you implement what you have learned.

Why you should use the Technical Notes

- They include extended explanations that did not fit into the book.
- You will find complete code examples, ready to compile and run.
- The document includes hardware diagrams, pin maps, and testing procedures.
- Each chapter's notes align with the topics covered, so you can learn **sequentially**.

How to Get Them

1. Visit: **www.sbblearning.com**
2. Enter the **chapter code** (mentioned at the end of each chapter) to access related files.
3. Download and explore, update your own local repository for practice.

Connecting With Me

- **Email:** [sbblearningauthor@gmail.com]
- **YouTube**: [www.youtube.com/@sbblearning-sateeshbaganal]

Reader Bonus:

If you have completed a chapter's exercises or implemented one of the example projects, share it with me! I regularly feature reader projects in my newsletter and may include them in future editions of my notes.

Remember, embedded systems development is not just about reading; it is about **building**. The technical notes are your bridge from theory to hands-on expertise.